ROCKIE

ROOKIE
The Story of a Season

by
JEROME WALTON

with
JIM LANGFORD

Diamond Communications, Inc.
South Bend, Indiana

1990

ROOKIE
Copyright © 1990
Jerome Walton and Jim Langford

Manufactured in the United States of America

DIAMOND COMMUNICATIONS, INC.
POST OFFICE BOX 88
SOUTH BEND, INDIANA 46624
(219) 287-5008

Library of Congress Cataloging-in-Publication Data

Walton, Jerome, 1965 -
    Rookie : the story of a season / by Jerome Walton with Jim
Langford.
        p.   cm.
    ISBN 0-912083-45-X : $18.95 -- ISBN 0-912083-44-1 : $8.95
    1. Walton, Jerome, 1965- . 2. Baseball players--United States-
-Biography. I. Langford,   Jim, 1937 -   II Title.
GV865.W35A3   1990
796.357'092--dc20
[B]   89-49283
                                                                        CIP

Contents

"Baseball is a rookie—
his experience no bigger than
the lump in his throat—
trying to begin the fulfillment of a dream."

—from *A Game For All America*
by Ernie Harwell

*For my son,
Jonathan Walton*

Preface

When Terry Sullivan, my attorney and personal representative, suggested back in August that I write a book, I have to say I liked the idea. For one thing, I could imagine the look on my high school English teacher's face when she heard that I was an author. But more important to me was that I could put in some permanent form all that had happened during a very special year in my life and an extraordinary season in the history of my team, the Chicago Cubs. It happened that my rookie season in the major leagues was also turning into an incredibly exciting four-team race for the division championship and, even though almost no one expected us to be, we were in the thick of it all season. That meant that I could tell my story and, at the same time, capture at least some of the drama and fun of a pennant race.

Working on the book during the last part of the season and on into October was a good experience for me. It let me focus on how blessed I have been with family, friends, good coaches, opportunity, and the ability that had to be there before it could be developed.

The book is about a year in my life when years of dreams and hard work came together in a way I will never forget. I hope it brings back to the readers thoughts of a season worth remembering.

Jerome Walton
November 1989

Acknowledgments

I want to thank my family, especially my mom, my late grandmom, my son Jonathan, and my girlfriend Tammy; my coaches Joe Jordan and Ronnie Powell, who taught me and believed in me; my friends who have been with me all the way; my coaches and managers in pro ball, especially Jim Tracy, Jim Essian, Jimmy Piersall, Don Zimmer; my teammates at each step along the way; and Cub fans who have made me feel welcome each time I take the field.

J.W.

I am grateful to Jill Langford, president of Diamond Communications, for her confidence that I was the right person to do this book with Jerome. As a lifelong Cub fan of very limited baseball talent, I was able to experience vicariously the thrill of running out to center field on Opening Day, the hard work and concentration needed to play the game well, the surprises and disappointments that unfold with the season, the sheer thrill and fun of a pennant race. I hope that I have helped at least some of that come through in the book. Jerome and I both wanted to seek a level where it would be interesting to fans and instructive to young players by filling its pages with baseball rather that bravado, bombast, or tabloid tidbits.

A number of people have been most helpful in supplying insights and materials, especially Mrs. Susie Hudson, Ms. Tammy Broom, and Jamie Cassady.

Mr. Terry Sullivan and Sheila Casserly of Terry Sullivan and Associates were not only the initiators of the project; they were enormously helpful in the interview stage of its development.

I thank also Ned Colletti, director of Media Relations for the Chicago Cubs, and Wanda Taylor of his staff; Bill Moor, sports editor of the *South Bend Tribune*; Rob Morton of the *Newnan Times-Herald*; Charles Singer of TV Sports Mailbag; photographer Stephen Green; Jeff Jeffers and Chuck Freeby of WNDU-TV in South Bend; Lance McAllister, Charlie Adams, Jon Thompson, Bob Lux, and Brett Kunz of South Bend's WSBT-TV and radio; Ann Pouk of Diamond Communications; Juanita Dix of J.D. Design; and Jeremy and Josh Langford for their support and encouragement.

Since Jerome doesn't make many errors, assume that any found here are mine.

J.R.L

 **Introduction**

Only longtime Cub fans or historians can really appreciate how unusual it is to have a great center-fielder wearing the home uniform in Wrigley Field. Search through the record books, study firsthand accounts through the decades, ask the oldest fans you can find, and then try to compile a list of candidates. The nominees are few, their playing days long gone. There are other positions where the Cubs have enjoyed stars from the beginning and still do: At first base—Anson, Chance, Grimm, Cavarretta, Banks, Buckner, and Grace, to name the most obvious. At second base, Evers, Hornsby, Herman, Hubbs, Beckert, and Sandberg, with a few others who did well for a few seasons in between the greats. And, over time, the Cubs have had some of the game's best catchers, third basemen, and short-stops. But there is no such tradition in center field at Wrigley.

Of all who labored there prior to 1940, only Bill Lange (1893-99) and Hack Wilson (1926-31) are enshrined in the Cubs' Hall of Fame and Hack is there mainly because of one year—1930—in which he hit 56 home runs and drove in 190 runs. The short, stocky Wilson was usually adequate in the field and he had a better than average arm, but it was not his fielding prowess that earned his place in history. Historians are quick to remind us that Hack was the goat of the 1929 World Series, missing two flyballs he probably should have caught in the infamous 10-run uprising staged by Connie Mack's Philadelphia Athletics in Game Four.

Thirteen years after Wilson was cast off to the Dodgers in 1931, the Cubs came up with Andy Pafko to patrol the middle of the outfield. In terms of combining offense and defense, Pafko may have been, until now, the best Cub ever at that position. In his nine seasons in Chicago, Andy hit .294, drove in 584 runs, and clubbed 126 homers. Equally important, he had good speed and a good arm. He, too, is in the Cubs' Hall of Fame. His lucky break came when Wid Matthews, general manager of the Cubs, traded him along with pitcher Johnny Schmitz, catcher Rube Walker, and second baseman Twig Terwilliger to Brooklyn for a sore-armed catcher named Bruce Edwards, 34-year-old Lefty Joe Hatten, reserve outfielder Gene Hermanski, and utility infielder Eddie Miksis. Pafko played left field on the pennant-winning Dodgers of 1952. The Cubs were left with a phrase, no doubt invented by Matthews: "Miksis will fix us." The trade made Matthews the laughingstock of the National League.

But never mind: For six years Sanquine Wid exuded optimism and sold pipe dreams. And it took his successor, John Holland, five years to bring some semblance of talent to and through the farm system. Even he couldn't come up with a centerfielder. In the years after Pafko, the Cubs opened the season with center field being patrolled by, in order, Hal Jeffcoat, Preston Ward, Bob Talbot, Gale Wade, Bob Will, Bobby Thomson, George Altman, Richie Ashburn, Al Heist, Lou Brock, Don Landrum, Billy Cowan, Billy Williams, Ty Cline, Adolfo Phillips, Don Young, Jim Hickman, Jose Ortiz, Rick Monday (for five years!), Jerry Morales, Greg Gross, Jerry Martin—well, you get the idea. Of those whose names you might recognize, Thomson and Ashburn were near the end of their careers, Brock and Williams were playing out of position, and only Rick Monday could be described as above average.

In 1984 we were treated to some fine center-field play by Bobby Dernier, who had a career year with the glove, at the bat, and on the bases. He fell off the following year but not all was lost. Dave Martinez played a very good center for one year and then was sent off to Montreal for Mitch Webster.

Forgive us if we had heard the praises of Jerome Walton as he came through the farm system and still reserved judgment. Forgive us for the sinking feeling we had when Walton dropped the first ball ever hit to him in the major leagues—an easy fly on Opening Day. But give us credit, too. It didn't take us long to recognize that this kid was different; his promise was real; his ability was stunning; his determination was contagious. Before the game was over on Opening Day, we knew we finally had a centerfielder, someone who would make good on all the I.O.U.'s left behind with the fans by those who had had temporary custody of center field at Wrigley since 1952.

Jerome Walton symbolized something else that was new at Wrigley—speed. The 1989 Cubs were arguably the fastest Cub team in history and Jim Frey and Don Zimmer deserve credit for going against the grain in letting that happen. The closeness of the power alleys at Wrigley, and the possibility that the wind would blow out more often than in, carved a rut out of which Cub general managers never seemed able to climb. Get the big guy who had the power to hit it out and the runs scored will more than compensate for a slow-footed defense.

To his credit, Dallas Green was probably the first Cub general manager to check the stopwatch before the slugging average. His immediate predecessor was Herman Franks, whose appearance in a uniform reflected his attitude toward speed.

When Green came to the Cubs, he was mystified as to how any organization could be so devoid of speed. He set about to correct the problem. To hurry things along, he acquired Ryne Sandberg and later Bob Dernier and Davey Lopes to offset the likes of Ron Cey and Keith Moreland.

It has only gotten better with time. In fact, the Cubs are now emphasizing power in at least some of the prospects they sign so that the system doesn't get out of balance with too much focus on speed. Meanwhile, Dawson, Walton, and Smith are in our outfield; Grace, Sandberg, Dunston, and Berryhill or Wrona all run well. If you want to know the difference it makes, ask the pitchers. Or better yet, remember the exciting season of 1989.

Well before spring training, Jim Frey had ignored the echoes of Lou Brock and traded popular Rafael Palmeiro, Jamie Moyer, and Drew Hall to the Texas Rangers for a wild reliever named Mitch Williams, a fourth starter named Paul Kilgus, a Double-A pitcher named Steve Wilson, and a utility infielder named Curtis Wilkerson. Frey's Cub jacket must be reinforced for flak because he stood fast by the deal, unflappably confident that it gave the Cubs what they needed.

The media howled, the fans voiced dismay, the players traded let loose on Frey and Zimmer, and a

Cub star even voiced an opinion about whether Palmeiro or Grace should have been the hitter traded. Zimmer wouldn't say much except that, going into spring training, he thought the team was stronger than it had been in 1988 and that his job was to do the best he could with what he had. Frey simply gave his enigmatic grin, like a card player who never bluffs and only bets from strength.

Spring began with lots of question marks. And ended with lots of question marks. Who would play in the outfield? Could Walton make the jump from Double-A? Could he hit .260? Who was going to play left?

The reports out of Mesa were strongly reminiscent of 1984 when weeks of dropped flyballs, no pitching, and a fight between Mel Hall and Dick Ruthven promised another year in the depths. But then, in the last week of spring camp, Green pulled off a trade that changed things around. Gary Matthews and Bob Dernier were instant starters and the Cubs were on their way.

In 1989 no such trade materialized. Amid speculation that Dave Winfield or Don Mattingly or possibly Darryl Strawberry or Dale Murphy would soon be in a Cub uniform, camp closed. Not even all of those who had been expected to make the team were on the plane headed north. Dwight Smith had a terrible spring and was sent to Iowa. Mike Harkey, counted on as the Cubs' fourth starter, found himself on the Iowa roster before spring camp broke up. So did Les Lancaster, who had enjoyed more than a few moments of better than average pitching in 1988.

Sportswriters had a field day. When the Cubs finished the exhibition season with a 9-23 record, wisecracks seemed to be the order of the day. Steve Wulf, writing in the special baseball issue of *Sports Illustrated*, was smug and confident in his pronouncement: "The Cubs, who haven't won a World Championship since 1908, have had only one winning season since 1972. You can be certain that this will not be their second." Chicago writers felt they were being generous to predict a finish as high as fourth for the Cubs. Later, it was revealed that on the eve of Opening Day, Jim Frey and Don Zimmer had agreed over dinner that a .500 season would be an acceptable performance. That didn't mean that they thought .500 was the promised land; it simply meant that, when you are coming off a 9-23 spring, .500 looks pretty good.

In writer Wulf's defense, one item in his writeup on the Cubs—who he predicted would finish fifth, ahead of the Phillies—turned out to be right on the mark. He had noted: "Zimmer will determine if Jerome Walton is ready for the majors and Walton will determine how good—or bad—the Cubs are this year."

An amazingly perceptive comment from someone who was so awestruck by the Mets that he went on record with the bizarre statement that, "Their [the Mets] bench and second-line pitching would probably finish fourth in the National League East." We all know who he had picked fifth.

But what made the writers so confident that the Cubs were so bad? They had led the league in batting average in 1988 and they boasted some bona fide all-star candidates at a number of positions. Damon Berryhill was regarded by scouts as one of the two best catchers in the league. Mark Grace had proven himself an outstanding hitter and defensive first baseman. Ryne Sandberg had no equal at second. Shawon Dunston, in spite of a poor second half, had shown that he was more than potential, especially in the field. Vance Law was coming off of the best year in his career. Andre Dawson was still an all-star performer in right field. That left only center and left as open questions and the signs were that Jerome Walton could certainly field the position as well as anyone and that Mitch Webster could play an adequate left field.

The glaring problem with the 1988 Cubs was the bullpen—which had acted more like arsonists than firemen all season long. With only 29 saves in 55 opportunities and a 4.40 ERA, the Cub bullpen had been the worst in baseball. The National League average was converting 72 percent of save opportunities. The Cubs' average was 53 percent. Clearly, Frey knew all of this and that's what impelled him to give up a very good hitter for a hard throwing, if wild, reliever. Further improvement could come by attrition—releasing Goose Gossage was a psychological lift for Cub fans and perhaps for the overall performance of the pen as well.

The starting pitching was not all that bad either. Greg Maddux and Rick Sutcliffe were among the top 20 in the league. Scott Sanderson showed promise in the spring that he was healed and ready to go; Mike Bielecki had done well in winter ball and in the spring; and Paul Kilgus had been a decent fourth starter with the Rangers. The ranks might be a little thin without Harkey, but who except the Mets was really rich in established pitching?

My point is simply that this was a better team than most writers thought it was. It is simply not true that they came from nowhere to win the division. Those writers who later excused their pre-season predictions by saying they had simply flunked chemistry, as though spirit by itself wins ball games, flunked honesty as well.

That is not to say that this team didn't have a character and spirit all its own. But spirit without talent doesn't win. The spirit of any team is an elusive quantity. It is real but intangible. When asked about the Notre Dame spirit, football coach Lou Holtz said, "Once I started to believe in it, it was real." Spirit of that kind doesn't precede winning; it develops along with winning. Once a team reaches beyond what is expected, the ceiling is raised; "We can do it" becomes a conviction instead of a hope. And, after it has been done, the team knows it can be done again. That kind of confidence is at the core of championship teams. As you read Jerome Walton's account of the 1989 season, you can see the confidence grow as the season progresses.

That confidence stayed alive in this team after the final out was recorded in the League Championship Series against the Giants. When it all ended, the Cubs were in the midst of a rally that simply fell short. One or two more hits and the Series would have moved back to Chicago. To a man the Cubs believed that, if they got the Giants back at Wrigley, Chicago would host the World Series. As you read this book, you know that 1989 was different from 1984; you get the sense that this team will be back again and again.

Rookie is the story of a remarkable year in the life of a young ballplayer who in one season went from Pittsfield in the Eastern League to Rookie of the Year in the National League. We do not intend the book to be a biography—Jerome is only 24 and most of his life lies ahead of him. Neither did we want it to be an exposé of life in the big leagues.

Instead, it is a book about the Cubs and their climb to the top of the National League East. It is about the desire, hard work, and confidence that enabled Jerome Walton to be the fuse that lit the Cubs' offense and, in his first season, one of the premier defensive centerfielders in the league. It is about baseball and, ultimately, it is about a ball-player and his formula for developing as a player and a person.

Jim Langford
Thanksgiving Day
November 23, 1989

1 Getting Started

When I think back on my childhood, I start counting my blessings. I never had to wonder whether I was loved and I never had reason to doubt that, if whatever I needed was within reach of my family, they would make sure that I got it. Even though both my mom and grandmom were divorced and my father left town for good when I was very young, my home was far from broken. I lived with my grandmom until I was 14. But my mom and stepdad lived only about three miles away and my grandpa lived nearby, too; so we saw each other all the time and it seemed as if I had more people encouraging me, taking care of me, and providing for me than most of the kids I knew. Newnan, Georgia is a nice town, about 40 miles southwest of Atlanta. It is predominantly white but, aside from the fact that there is still a chapter of the Ku Klux Klan in town, there aren't really that many racial tensions. I've always found that playing sports is a good way to get along with everybody. Members of my family were all good athletes and I guess it was natural that I grew up loving sports. My grandmom was a real Braves fan. I remember lots of times in the summer when we'd watch the Braves together on TV and, when the game was over, I'd go out in the yard and toss rocks up in the air and hit them with a stick. Like most kids I'd pretend to be a star coming through with a hit to win the game. Most of the time I pretended to be Dale Murphy. Sometimes my family would take me to Atlanta for a Braves game. I'll never forget being in the stands the night Hank Aaron hit his record-breaking 715th home run. You never forget the team you grow up with and a part of me will always be rooting for the Braves.

I started playing organized ball in Little League when I was eight years old. My mom would pick me up and drive me to practice and to the games. I told my mom that I didn't want a cheap glove, that I needed a good one. She bought me a beauty, almost too much glove for my hand. I loved that glove and I still have it at home. I played for Brenda's in the AA League and my mom saved the newspaper clippings describing games like the one where we beat Lambert, 19-18, and another where we lost to Southside, 15-14. I hit .538 that season and, more importantly, had a lot of fun. I was a catcher in Little League, then I switched to third base and pitcher in Babe Ruth League and that's what I played in high school, too.

When I was 14, my grandmom died of cancer. It seemed like it hit her all at once, but at least she didn't suffer a lot. She had been like a second mother to me. She gave me what I wanted—mainly the freedom to play sports to my heart's content—but she didn't spoil me. It was really hard to lose her and I wish she had lived long enough to see me play in the big leagues, but her memory is with me all the time.

I moved in with my mom and stepdad and had to

adjust to a whole new set of rules; but they were great about letting me go out for the Newnan High teams in three sports. On the freshman football team I played split end, running back, quarterback, and safety on defense. I was a varsity starter as a sophomore and I played well enough in high school to attract the interest of some college recruiters. I was good at guard and forward on the basketball team and I averaged about 21 points per game in high school. I was only about 5'10" and 155 pounds, but I was always blessed with good speed. I think I could have played major college basketball, but baseball was still my favorite sport.

I was lucky to have Coach Joe Jordan as a high school baseball coach. He had been an assistant coach at Jacksonville State College before coming to Newnan, and he really knows baseball. In my senior year, Coach Jordan talked to me about what I planned to do after graduation. I told him that I'd had some college scholarship offers for football and basketball and that I really wanted to get a college education. Coach told me that he thought I could make it with professional baseball in a couple of years and he offered to take me over to Enterprise, Alabama for a tryout with Ronnie Powell, the coach of Enterprise State Junior College. I jumped at Coach's offer.

When we got to Enterprise I put on my uniform and then did some drills and sprints and fielded some balls at third. Then Coach Powell told me he already had a third baseman who was transferring to Enterprise State from a four-year school and he asked if I had ever played the outfield. I told him I hadn't and he told me to go out to center field so he could hit me some flyballs. I did and the first one he hit was way over my head. Almost by instinct I turned and headed deep and put my glove up in time to catch it. When I went home that day, I knew I'd be going to college. That summer I had a job with a construction company doing concrete work. I was really looking forward to going to school.

Even though I had a scholarship, I had to pay for room and board. My grandfather helped with that; otherwise I probably wouldn't have been able to go. I took hard classes because I was trying to get a good education. I wanted to do my best, especially in English and Math, which were my favorite subjects. It helped that Coach Powell encouraged his players to remember that books were more important than baseball. But when you were on the baseball field you knew that he wasn't just a coach, he was a teacher—and a perfectionist.

I had raw talent coming out of high school, but Coach Powell is the one who really worked with me to develop it. He had played college ball under Eddie Stanky, who was a smart, hardnosed major league infielder and later manager. From what I hear, Stanky was the kind of player who knew the game inside and out and who would always find a way to win. Coach Powell was that way, too. He taught us to concentrate on the game, to be aggressive. He'd say, "If you're behind on the count and the pitch is inside, turn into it and let it hit you." When a breaking ball came in close and you had two strikes on you, if you *didn't* get hit, you heard about it! He wanted you to get on base. We won a game like that: we had the bases loaded and one of our players took a fastball in the back to drive in the winning run in the state tournament.

Coach Powell was tough, but he was also like a brother to the players. He taught the basic skills and the fine points and he worked us hard until we got them. He taught us never to be satisfied, never to think that we didn't need to improve. He could take a hoodlum off the street and make a person out of him. And even if the players on our team weren't hoodlums, we were mostly players that no other school had wanted. Coach Powell loves baseball and hates to lose. He'd get on your case but you always knew that he was working to make you not only a better player but a better person as well.

If it sounds like I'm giving Coach Powell a lot of credit for the good things that have developed in my life and my career, I am doing exactly that. He didn't lose confidence in me even though in my freshman year I finished with a batting average of .190. My mechanics were simply messed up and there really wasn't enough time to work with them in the midst of the season. At the end of the season, Coach told me to open up my stance so that I wouldn't step in the bucket; he taught me how to adjust my approach to the ball so I would stay on it instead of pulling off of it.

That summer I worked out a lot at a school up the hill from my mom's house. I'd put a ball on the tee and, using my open stance, I'd hit a bag of balls and then chase them and start over. When I went back to school in the fall, I was ready to show Coach Powell that my "funky" stance, as he called it, was going to help my hitting. He pitched batting practice to me and I hit him pretty well.

When the 1985 fall season opened against Troy State, a Division II baseball power, I drove an outside fastball off the right-field wall for a double. Then, when they tried to back me off with an inside fastball, I hit it out of the park. Unorthodox or not, I figured to stay with the open stance as long as it worked for me. Coach Powell agreed. A week later our team went to Pensacola, Florida to play a twi-night double-header—the first game against Southeastern Louisiana University and the second against Spring Hill

College. Coach told us that major league scouts would be there because our games were just part of a multi-team tournament that gave them a chance to evaluate a lot of players in just a few days.

Coach Powell played all freshmen in the first game. I watched along with the other sophomores and we could see the scouts with their notepads and stopwatches. By the time we got our chance to play in the second game, most of the scouts had left. Earl Winn of the Chicago Cubs and Mark Weidemaier of the California Angels were the only ones left.

I opened the game with a bunt hit. Coach Powell had a standing rule that, if you couldn't bunt, you wouldn't play on his team. He spent hours teaching us how to bunt, working on it with us, challenging us to try to be the best bunter on the team. Sometimes he'd mark a spot on the third-base line and we'd compete to see who could drop the ball closest to it. I guess the scouts had timed me running to first and also liked the fact that I always sprinted to and from center field. Coach asked me if I'd be willing to run the 60-yard dash for Earl Winn after the game. It was about 1:30 in the morning when the game ended. Then the scout measured off the distance and I ran it. I slipped when I started but still made it in 6.5 seconds.

When the fall season ended, I had a pretty good idea that I was going to be drafted in the upcoming January 1986 draft. The Angels told me that they were going to draft me in the first round, but later they said they were going to go for a pitcher and that they would pick me in the second round. The Cubs beat them to it. Chicago picked a pitcher named Shawn Boskie in the first round and then selected me in the second, when their turn came before the Angels. I batted against the pitcher the Angels chose over me when we were both in A ball. It gave me a special pleasure when I hit him hard.

Even though I had been drafted, I couldn't sign a professional contract until after the spring season of my sophomore year. Using my open stance, I had a great season. I hit .439 with 24 stolen bases. I also pitched when I was needed and had a 6-1 record on the mound. Although I was clocked in the low 90s, I usually had a sore shoulder after pitching. Back in high school, I had separated my right shoulder in a football game and it simply hadn't healed properly. Our team finished with a 30-13 record and we won the division championship. It was a nice ending to my college career to be named Most Valuable Player in the Southern Junior College Conference.

As soon as the season was over, the Cubs got in touch with me with a contract offer. Had I not signed with them, I would have been eligible for the draft again in June. I signed for $24,000, including incentives. The first actual check was for $15,000 and it came to the house the day after I left to report to the Cubs in Mesa, Arizona.

A week or so before, the Cubs had sent me a mimeographed information package, addressed "Dear Ballplayer." It had a nice ring to it. The material pointed out that only one in 40,000 amateur players is fortunate enough to get the opportunity to sign a contract, that professional baseball offers a lot of benefits like professional instruction, a long off-season, life insurance, and major medical benefits, and the opportunity to learn poise under pressure. In addition, as if anyone would need more incentive, it stated that if you made it to the major league level, you would have an opportunity through hard work to become wealthy by using your skills.

The material then went on to spell out what was going to happen next. All newly-signed players from the January or June draft were to report to a minicamp in Mesa, Arizona before being assigned to one of the short-season farm teams, either at Wytheville, Virginia in the Appalachian League or at Geneva, New York in the New York-Penn League. It said that transportation to Arizona, to the assigned club, and back home at the end of the season would be paid for by the Cubs; housing and meals were to be picked up during training in Arizona; daily meal money was paid on road trips; players were responsible for their own housing arrangements in their assigned city; all first-year players made the same monthly salary of $700; and you had to supply your own glove and shoes. The uniform, hat, and bats would be furnished by the club.

Getting on the plane in Atlanta for Arizona was exciting for me because it was the first time I'd ever flown. And also because I was heading off to see if I could make a dream come true.

2 The Minors

I reported to HoHoKam Park in Mesa with all of the other rookies and I was more anxious than I was nervous. I didn't know anybody and I was kind of homesick at first. I really missed my family. I had married my high school girlfriend, Cindy, near the end of high school and we had a son named Jonathan. They were my family and I was hoping to do well for them. I had never been that far away from home before. But there were a few guys there from Alabama and at least we had a little geography in common.

Our job in Arizona was to take instruction—much of it individual—on the basics of hitting, fielding, and running. I knew that what had attracted Earl Winn and the Cubs to sign me was my speed and hustle, but I also knew that Coach Powell had given me a very sound foundation in how to play baseball. Almost from the moment he had hit me fungo flies during my tryout, he worked hard with me to develop my defensive skills as a centerfielder.

18

I was lucky because our home field at Enterprise State was large enough to give us a good idea of the kind of territory you have to cover in the outfield once you reach professional ball. It was 330 feet down the foul lines, 365 feet in the power alleys, and 395 feet to dead center. Coach Powell taught us that speed is important, but that the most important step for an outfielder is the first one—you have to break in the right direction. Good defense requires good instincts, but the best instincts are the ones that are honed by practice and experience. It is a lot more complex than it looks. You have to know the hitter's tendencies. Does he pull the ball or go to the opposite field? How fast is he? If he's slow, you can play him a little deeper. What is the count? If he's behind on the count, he's less likely to pull than he is to protect himself. Finally, what does your pitcher throw? The fence, the wind, and the sun can affect how a ball should be played. Coach Powell used to make the outfielders stay for extra work on windy days and he taught us how to use sunglasses to lessen the difficulties on bright days.

I didn't go to Arizona thinking that I knew it all, but I did go with good habits which Coach had drilled into me. And with the confidence he gave me that I could play this game.

When rookie camp broke up, the two squads headed to their respective cities and we were ready for our first professional competition.

Wytheville is a small town of less than a thousand people, up in the mountains of Virginia. It is a very pretty place, even though there is not a whole lot to do for entertainment. The bus trips to other towns in the Southern Division of the league were usually along mountain roads to places such as Elizabethton, Johnson City, Kingsport, and Bristol. Eight of us roomed together in a two-story house that we rented. We mostly cooked for ourselves because we really couldn't afford to eat out very often. But we had a good time. The meal money wasn't much and the pay wasn't good, but I was making a living playing baseball and, from the time I was eight years old, that's what I wanted to do.

We played 68 games in the short season and won 22 of them. Derrick May had a good season, hitting .320, third best in the league. I'm not sure why, but at Wytheville I closed up my stance again. Even though the open stance had been very successful the year before in college, I guess I figured that since no one else hit that way I probably should square off more and close my stance a bit. I was second in runs scored (48), 10th in batting (.288), and third in stolen bases (21). I was named the league's Player of the Month for July and I made the league All-Star team. I was glad to be able to call home with that kind of news.

At the end of the season at Wytheville, I was told to report to Arizona for the Instructional League. It was fun because players were there from every level of the Cubs' system. It was also good because it gave me a chance to sharpen my skills and get more at-bats. It is great for helping a player make real progress because you get lots of coaching and as much practice as you want. I got to work with Jimmy Piersall and he really knows his stuff. You respect someone who's trying to teach you how to play the outfield when you know he was such a great out-fielder himself.

Once Instructional League was over, it was time to go home and find a job for the winter. I went back to my job with the construction company and worked out with weights and ran to stay in shape. My next step was going to Peoria in the Class A Midwest League.

When you are trying to work your way up through the minors, you have to be careful not to be impatient. You want to go as far and as fast as your skills will take you, but you don't want to lose your concentration by looking beyond where you are and what you need to do to succeed at the level you are at right then.

I was glad to leave my winter job and get back to baseball in March. I reported to the Cubs' minor league complex in Mesa. I decided to open up my stance again and I think it improved my hitting. Richie Zisk, the Cubs' hitting instructor, wanted me to close it, but I decided to stay with it and get comfortable with it. I really think it helps me see the ball better and to stay on it instead of pulling off of it. There is a kind of readiness that goes with this stance. When you're opened up like that, I think you can really attack the ball. For whatever reason, I couldn't attack it as well when I was more squared up. My point is, if you try a stance and you like it and it works for you, stay with it.

Peoria, Illinois is a great city. The people there are really nice and the team had outstanding management. The Midwest League is a good league. We finished second in the Southern Division with a 71-69 record and more than 195,000 fans paid to see us play. I lived near Bradley University in a furnished apartment that I shared with Heathcliff Slocumb, who was one of our top pitchers. With rent to pay and a car payment to make plus the need to send money home, I couldn't ever get far enough ahead to save anything.

During the course of the year, my wife and I went through a divorce. That's not an easy experience for anyone and it wasn't for me. Coach Powell had taught us that when something is wrong off the field, you deal with it when you get off the field. I had to put the whole thing out of my mind during the games. But afterwards, my main concern was to make sure that Jonathan was okay and that I'd be able to see him as much as possible.

I think I became a better ballplayer at Peoria. I really started getting comfortable with my open stance and there was a period of a week or so when my approach to the ball was almost exactly the way I wanted it to be. To this day I use the tape of my at-bats during that stretch as the model for what I should be doing. I used it in Peoria, too, whenever my hitting fell off. There was one stretch where I was in a slump for almost two weeks. I asked Jim Tracy, our manager, to work with me on it. We watched the tapes of when I was going well and my recent at-bats when I wasn't. Then he would come to the park early to throw me extra batting practice and suggest alterations in my stride. It was Jim who noticed that, instead of stepping toward the plate in my stride, I was stepping toward the pitcher. Once he pointed that out, I was able to make the proper adjustment and start hitting again. Jim also was the one who gave me the nickname, "Juice."

In a sense that is one of the key differences between amateur and professional ball. In college, Coach Powell was watching his players all the time, correcting their mistakes and working with them to improve every aspect of their play. In the pros it is much less personal than that. You are really on your own. If you have developed good work habits, this is when it pays off. Having talent by itself isn't enough to make it in the pros. You have to know how to work on your hitting, fielding, and running and to use your practice time, especially batting practice, efficiently.

One of the games I remember best from my season in Peoria was Jeff Schwartz's 4-0 no-hitter against Kenosha on July 10. With one out in the ninth, the Kenosha batter drove a line drive into the gap. I went after it with everything I had, dove and came up with the ball. The umpire signaled that the batter was out, but to this day I think I might have trapped it. Another one of our pitchers, Pat Gomez, gave the outfielders a rest when he struck out 18 Wausau batters in a game on May 3.

After games like these there is always a lot of extra kidding and fun in the minor leagues. As I've said, the pay and the meal money are barely enough to get by on and the bus rides are long and boring, but it's still worth it. You learn how to live pretty closely with the different kinds of people on the team and to get along in rather cramped space and less than luxurious conditions. You're in it because you love the game of baseball and you're chasing a dream. The movie *Bull Durham* was right on the mark in showing how players in the minors work and hope for the day they'll get a chance to be in a major league game. The fans who come out to see games in the minor leagues are there because they really love baseball too. Over the course of a season you get to know some of the faces and voices in the stands. The fans in Peoria were really terrific. They helped to make my year with the Chiefs one I'll never forget. My totals told me that I could play well at this level. I hit .335 with 24 doubles, 11 triples, and six homers. I scored 102 runs and stole 49 bases. I made the mid-season and post-season Midwest League All-Star teams. I had a feeling when I left Peoria after the season to report to Mesa for the Instructional League that I'd be promoted to Double-A ball.

By the time I reported to spring training in 1988 I had been assigned to Pittsfield, Massachusetts in the Double-A Eastern League. Others promoted from Peoria included catcher Kelly Mann and pitchers Steve Parker and Mike Harkey. Coming to

Pittsfield from Winston-Salem, the Cubs' A team in the Carolina League, were catcher Joe Girardi, outfielders Ced Landrum, Johnny Lewis, and Mike Tullier, and pitchers Jeff Hirsch, Bill Kazmierczak, Joe Kramer, Kris Roth, and Dean Wilkins, among others. We were replacing some pretty good ballplayers who had been promoted from Pittsfield to the Iowa Cubs in the Triple-A American Association. Among that group were Mark Grace, who only stayed in Iowa for 21 games before he was called up to the Cubs, outfielders Doug Dascenzo, Rolando Roomes, and Dwight Smith, catcher Rick Wrona, and pitchers Len Damian, Jeff Pico, and Dave Masters. No wonder the 1987 Pittsfield Cubs finished first by 11 games!

But we turned out to be a pretty good team, too. We finished the regular season 12 games over .500, but lost to Vermont in the playoffs. We had pitching—our team ERA was 2.95. We had speed—Ced Landrum stole 69 bases, Rich Amaral 54, and I had 42 of the team's total 248. We had hitting—I won the batting title with a .331 average and my teammates Bryan House and Hector Villanueva were second and third with .316 and .314 averages. And we had defense—Joe Girardi threw out 55 baserunners and our starting outfielders made a total of only 13 errors. Even though we played good ball, we didn't draw very well in attendance. That might be one of the reasons why the Cubs moved their Double-A team to Charlotte of the Southern League.

I had a couple of special thrills in my season at Pittsfield. I had a triple and the game-winning single in the Eastern League All-Star game. More importantly, I worked hard to sharpen my defensive game. I finished with a .993 fielding average, having made two errors in 283 chances. It was just by luck that Jim Frey happened to be in the stands on the night of July 27 when I threw out three runners at the plate. I got another one the next night. He didn't say anything directly to me about it, but I figured he'd seen me at my best and that I hadn't done anything to hurt my chances for promotion. And my guess is that Jim Essian, our manager, told the Cubs that I was ready for a close look the next spring.

In my three seasons in the minors, I had a .324 batting average and 112 stolen bases. I heard some talk that I would be called up to the Cubs for a look in September, but it didn't happen.

What did happen was that the Cubs told me that they wanted me to play winter ball in the Dominican Republic. Actually, I was glad they did because I wanted to go. I needed to make some money over the winter and winter ball on an island was better than concrete work anywhere, anytime. Plus, I knew that if I did well in winter ball, I'd have a chance to be put on the Cubs' 40-man roster. Finally, it was a chance to get some more experience, to face more pitching—some of it from guys who were already at the major league or Triple-A level.

I took a flight into Santo Domingo and it was the first time I had been to a foreign country. I was assigned to San Cristobal and two other Cub farmhands, infielder Brian Guinn and pitcher Fernando Zarranz, were on that team with me. I had heard that three more pitchers from the Cubs' system were going to be with us, too, but apparently they got assigned elsewhere. I know it sounds funny—especially because I was a pitcher myself part of the time in college—but since I've been in pro ball, I don't hang around much with pitchers. I like them all right as people, but they tend to hang out together, work with their own coach, and do things differently than the position players do. I read somewhere that Frank Robinson said the hardest part of managing for him is handling the pitchers. He says that there is a natural distance between hitters and pitchers and that he didn't know any good hitter, himself included, who ever felt like a pitcher was a friend. I'm not sure I'd go that far, but I tend to stay away from them.

We lived in a very nice hotel in the D.R. I stayed in the hotel a great deal because I didn't know Spanish and I couldn't really communicate with anybody. When I went anywhere, it was usually with someone who was good with the language. I had trouble getting used to the food until I settled on a diet of rice and pork chops and I decided to have that every day.

Most of the players in the winter league are either young major leaguers or players in the minor leagues in the States. The rest are native Dominican players who are hoping to get noticed and land a contract. Baseball is a passion with the Dominicans and, when you think about all the players who have made it to the major leagues from the Dominican Republic, it almost seems that they were born to play the game— especially at shortstop. Maybe part of the extra motivation comes from the desire to become good enough to play in the States and escape the poverty back there. I was told that there is even more poverty in Haiti; but it's nasty in the D.R. It was a shock to see little kids in rags sleeping outside on the streets. Maybe the fans who come to the games are looking for something to distract them for a few hours from the toughness of their lives. Whatever it is, they are wild fans. If you're an outfielder over there, you have to keep half an eye on the stands; they throw everything at you from garbage to beer bottles. I made four or five errors during the season because the field was terrible. That's when I was especially careful to dodge whatever was coming my way from the stands.

It didn't help the overall mood of the Caimanes fans that our team finished in last place with a 22-30 record, 11 games behind Licey. I hit .298. I don't know exactly when the Cubs decided to put me on their 40-man major league roster for the spring of 1989, whether playing winter ball had helped or whether the trade that sent Rafael Palmeiro to Texas meant they were going to turn to their farm system to see who could fill the vacancy in the outfield. All I knew was that, after Andre Dawson and Mitch Webster, there were six outfielders competing for three spots and that I was one of the six. I couldn't wait for spring training.

3 Spring Training 1989

Even though I had seen or heard my name mentioned as a possible answer to what the Cubs were going to do to fill the spot in the outfield left by the trade of Palmeiro to the Rangers, I didn't go to Mesa with a burden on my back. I didn't really feel that the pressure was on me as much as it was on those who had been up with the Cubs before and who were now trying to win a spot on the roster again. Gary Varsho had played in 46 games, Doug Dascenzo in 26, Darrin Jackson in 100 with the Cubs in 1988. Dwight Smith, Derrick May, and I were the three who had never been there before.

I figured that time was on my side in the sense that I had never played in the major leagues and, in fact, I had never even played in Triple-A ball. So, when I got to Mesa, I wasn't really nervous; I just wanted to do the best I could and see what happened.

From the start, the veteran players were terrific to all of the rookies; they didn't ignore us, or shy away from us, or treat us like newcomers. I had always dreamed about what it would be like coming into a major league locker room for the first time. And when it happened, I still felt like I was dreaming. There I was with all of the superstars and I couldn't believe it. I just shook my head and said to myself, "Is this really happening? Am I really in this locker room, or what?" That might seem uncool or simple, but when you're on the same roster with people such as Andre Dawson, Ryne Sandberg, and Rick Sutcliffe, you're with people who have already proved what they can do. Being cool isn't what you think of. My locker was between Scott Sanderson and Curt Wilkerson. They, like everybody else, made me feel welcome. I had met Sanderson when he came down to the Instructional League to work on overcoming some problems with his back, but I don't think he remembered me. Well, what do you expect? He's a pitcher, after all.

Players today don't go to spring training to work off excess weight from winter or to tone up muscles that they haven't used since the previous fall. I've read that a lot of players needed to do that 20 or 30 years ago. But now, with major league salaries at a level where most players don't have to find winter jobs selling clothes or whatever, staying in shape year 'round is part of being a ballplayer. You do calisthenics. These are mainly to stretch out and fine tune the muscles you use running and throwing. You work with weight equipment and generally use the off-season to get yourself physically ready for the new season.

This means that you can spend the five or six weeks at spring training working on getting your timing down, trying a new pitch, reviewing basic plays, learning the signs, and other things that get you ready for the season. The exhibition season opens in early March and that gives the manager and coaches a chance to evaluate players and work on plays in game conditions. We had 32 games scheduled from March 3 to the 31st against other teams that train in Arizona: the Giants, A's, Brewers, Angels, Indians, Padres, and Mariners. Then those who made the 24-man roster would go up to Minnesota for two games in early April before the real season opened.

Even though I'd much rather win than lose anytime, the exhibition games are not really a true test of how good a team is or can be. You're basically learning to play together as a team and waiting for your pitchers to get their best stuff working. As long as I can remember I have always thrived on competition. I've never looked at a new challenge as a possible failure; reaching higher or being in the thick of it when everything is on the line is a really good way to test yourself, measure yourself, and extend yourself.

Within limits, I do set goals for myself. When spring training started, I had as my goal to play as well as I could and to show that I could play at the major league level. Those goals were within my reach and my control. I didn't go to camp with the goal of being the Cubs' starting centerfielder on Opening Day because other elements beyond my control could have blocked that goal from being reached, at least this year.

Since my college days, I have always used practice time with specific purposes in mind: improving my bunting, pulling the ball, hitting to right, cutting my time on the bases, perfecting throws to the cutoff man, and so forth. I think a ballplayer knows what he can do and in that sense he should set his own standards and not those that are set for him by other people, whether it's the manager, the press, or the fans. Don Zimmer let me know that he felt that way too. He told me not to press or be anxious and that I'd be in the major leagues before long, even if it didn't happen on Opening Day this season.

Still, I knew the Cubs were giving me a good shot at it right here and now. I had read in the paper that Zim was asking other people in the organization about me and getting their opinions even before spring training started. Jimmy Piersall told Zim that I could play defense with the best centerfielders in the National League and that I might hit about .260. Rickie Zisk agreed that I could probably hit .250 or .260.

I think Zim wanted to see for himself whether I would be overmatched against big league pitching. I think what was going to decide it for him was not that I absolutely had to put in a year in Triple-A ball—Zim doesn't live by these unspoken rules—but whether I was ready mentally for the major leagues, whether I could play under control and under pressure, whether I could keep my confidence and concentration in good times and bad. Thanks especially to my college coach, I learned those things a few years before and had been working on them ever since.

Zim put me in the lineup. I was glad for a chance to prove that I could hit big league pitching. I had some reasons to be confident. I had hit for a good average in the minor leagues and, even down there, you'll find pitchers who throw in the 90s and who have good breaking stuff. I was finding out that the main difference between the pitching I was used to and the pitching I was seeing in the spring was that up here the pitchers have more command of their stuff; they can pitch to spots, throw the curve or a slider even when they're behind on the count, change speeds, and work the corners consistently.

When I read that what I had to do to earn the starting job with the Cubs was to hit .260, I thought to myself, "I can *bunt* 260." I wasn't being overconfident; I just figured I could make whatever adjustments I had to make and that that would be easier the more I got to hit against big league pitching. I also knew that the bunt was one of my best weapons. A couple of years before, during the winter, I had worked out at Braves Stadium in Atlanta, along with some guys, Brett Butler among them. He is one of the best bunters in the game and he talked to me about how important it could be in my game since I had the speed and the bat control to do it well. I'll always be grateful to Coach Powell for the hours spent making us bunt until we could do it in our sleep.

We all got along well as a team in spring training; the atmosphere was friendly and guys were always joking around and kidding one another. People started calling me by my nickname "Juice" and I felt like I belonged. All of the young players and the non-roster players like Domingo Ramos and Dave Owen knew pretty much when the cuts were going to come. Every time I survived a cut, I called home and talked to Jonathan and my mom and my girlfriend, Tammy. I told them I was going to make the team.

On March 20, my close friend Dwight Smith was optioned to Iowa. Dwight just had a bad spring. Some players might have let themselves get down or find someone to blame for the fact they were cut, but Dwight didn't take it that way. He just said that he hadn't played well and that he'd go to Iowa, work hard, and come back. A lot of the game of baseball is mental. Not in the sense that you have to be thinking all the time—you can do too much of that. If you try to concentrate on concentrating, you'll probably lose your concentration. It's mental in terms of attitudes. Dwight didn't make excuses; he went to Iowa to work, especially on his fielding. He's always been a great hitter and his fielding improved a lot by the time he came back to the Cubs in May. Derrick May was sent to Charlotte. He's a really good hitter,too, and he'll make it in the big leagues before long.

As we went into the last week of the exhibition schedule, it was time for paring down the roster further. Doug Dascenzo, Mike Harkey, Les Lancaster, and Dean Wilkins were sent to Iowa on March 26. Then I knew for sure I had made the team. Right after that Zim called me into his office and told me that I was his starting centerfielder. I can't begin to express how good that felt. I called home and told my family to come to Chicago for Opening Day.

Our team wasn't exactly burning up the Cactus League in Arizona. Even so, I found out firsthand about Cub fans. We played to a capacity crowd every day and, even though we lost 23 of 30 games in Arizona, they didn't throw anything at us. In fact, we drew more than 126,000 fans to HoHoKam Park, the best spring training attendance of any major league team. There were a couple of predictions made in Mesa that probably seemed farfetched. Mike Bielecki told the press that the Cubs would be playing the Baltimore Orioles in the World Series. And I told my attorney Terry Sullivan and his assistant Sheila Casserly that I was going to be Rookie of the Year. I set that as a goal, despite the fact that the media all seemed to say that the best any rookie could hope for this year was to finish second to Gregg Jefferies of the Mets. Of course, that's the same media that thought the Mets should print playoff tickets over the winter.

One of the things that is new for a rookie is the amount of media attention that goes with being a big league ballplayer. Sometimes things appear in the paper that are taken out of context and blown up into being something they aren't. A big issue was made of something Andre was supposed to have said about the Palmeiro trade, to the effect that Rafael was a better hitter than Mark Grace. The media looked to stir something up between Andre and Mark, but the two straightened it out themselves and the other guys on the team ignored it.

The last two exhibition games were against the Twins at the Metrodome on April 1 and 2. The way we played in those games made it look like the real April Fool's joke was on all the writers who had decided that we weren't a very good team. I said after those two games that we had a good ball club here. It was my first year in the major leagues and I really didn't know how good the other teams were; but I felt that we would score some runs and play good defense and, if our pitching staff was good, we'd be a real solid club.

I think some of our veterans weren't quite sure what to expect this season. Rick Sutcliffe said that this was the first time he could remember not being able to predict who would be on the roster before spring training even began. And Andre was quoted as saying he just didn't know how far this team could go, how good it could be. Zim admitted later that he and Jim Frey had agreed right before we went to Chicago for Opening Day that, given the number of young players in key positions on the roster, a .500 season would be decent. At that point, people were talking about the Cubs and White Sox both finishing last. A writer in *Sports Illustrated* seemed very sure we were headed nowhere. He wrote: "The Cubs, who haven't won a World Championship since 1908, have had only one winning season since 1972. You can be certain this will not be their second." The poll of baseball experts in *The Sporting News* assigned us to fifth place, with only the Phillies behind us. Of the 186 writers polled, 155 gave the Eastern Division title to the Mets. It was almost like people were feeling sorry for us because we played for the Cubs. But we didn't agree with that stuff. We had six or seven starting position players back from the previous season in which the Cubs had the best team batting average in the league. They just didn't have a good bullpen. And that is why Jim Frey went out and got Mitch Williams.

For a team that was supposed to be so bad, we sure didn't act like all was lost. Nobody was down when we left spring training. Nobody was acting like the world was ending or we had been sentenced to a terrible season. Everybody was happy and having fun. I can't remember one time then or into the season when the mood was so down that people were hanging their heads and forgetting how to kid or be kidded.

Fifteen of the 24 players on the Opening Day roster were not with the Cubs on Opening Day in 1988 and five of us were rookies: Joe Girardi, Phil Stephenson, Steve Wilson, Rick Wrona, and myself. Joe, Steve, and I had all been in Double-A ball a year ago.

What was it like getting on the bus for the airport and the plane that would take us to Chicago? I felt like I was a major leaguer. My dream was coming true and, if I got to play in one game in the major leagues, that dream would be realized in a way that nothing could ever change and no one could ever take away from me. I thought about my family and my coaches and I couldn't wait for Opening Day.

4 Starting for the Cubs

April 4

I don't think even my dreams had prepared me for what it was really like to be the starting center-fielder for the Cubs on Opening Day. I wasn't scared so much as I was awed by it all. The whole atmosphere was unlike anything I'd ever experienced. You could tell that all the players were excited on Opening Day; it was kind of electric. When we finished batting practice and went into the clubhouse, the fans who had come early were just sort of milling around; some kids were at the wall near the dugout trying to get autographs, and a few people were yelling encouragement to guys such as Ryno, Mark, and Andre.

When we came out for the introduction and National Anthem, the park was jammed full. I ran out to my position in center field and I felt like the whole world, or a good portion of it, was around me. I don't remember the first pitch. I was looking up at the crowd and then I realized that Rick had already thrown a pitch. I'm glad the batter didn't hit it to me.

36

Cubs 5, Phillies 4

	ab	r	h	bi		ab	r	h	bi
Dernier cf	5	0	2	0	Walton cf	4	0	2	1
Herr 2b	5	0	1	0	Webster lf	4	0	1	0
Hayes 1b	4	1	1	0	Sandberg 2b	4	1	2	1
Schmidt 3b	5	1	1	1	Dawson rf	3	1	1	2
C. James lf	5	0	1	0	Grace 1b	4	0	2	0
R. Jones rf	3	1	2	0	Law 3b	3	0	0	0
G.A. Harris p	0	0	0	0	Dunston ss	3	1	0	0
Parrett p	0	0	0	0	Girardi c	3	1	2	0
Ford ph	1	0	0	0	Sutcliffe p	2	1	2	0
McWilliams p	0	0	0	0	S.Wilson p	0	0	0	0
Ryal 1b	1	0	0	0	Schiraldi p	1	0	0	0
Thon ss	2	0	0	0	M.Williams	1	0	0	0
Daulton c	1	1	1	1					
Jordan 1b	1	0	1	2					
Bedrosian p	0	0	0	0					
Youmans p	2	0	0	0					
Lake c	2	0	0	0					
Totals	**37**	**4**	**10**	**4**	**Totals**	**32**	**5**	**12**	**4**

Philadelphia	000	012	010—4
CUBS	001	211	00x—5

E—Girardi, Walton. DP—Philadelphia 3. LOB—Philadelphia 11, CUBS 7. 2B—Sandberg, Grace. HR—Dawson (1), Daulton (1), Schmidt (1).

	IP	H	R	ER	BB	SO
Philadelphia						
Youmans L,0-1	5	9	4	4	1	3
G.A. Harris	1/3	1	1	1	1	0
Parrett	1 2/3	1	0	0	0	0
McWilliams	1/3	1	0	0	0	0
Bedrosian	2/3	0	0	0	2	0
CUBS						
Sutcliffe W, 1-0	5 2/3	5	3	3	3	4
S. Wilson	0	1	0	0	0	0
Schiraldi	1 2/3	1	1	0	0	0
M. Williams S,1	1 2/3	3	0	0	2	3

S. Wilson pitched to 1 batter in the 6th.
BK—Parrett, M. Williams
Umpires—Home, Froemming; First, Tata; Second, DeMuth; Third,Rippley.
T—3:06 A—33,661

It might have looked as though I was still looking at the crowd when I dropped Mike Schmidt's easy flyball in the second inning for my first major league error, but that wasn't what happened. I was playing him deep out of respect for his power. He took one of those big swings and hit the ball off the end of the bat and I simply misjudged it. I broke back and then had to move in fast and the ball hit off the heel of my glove. Still, I'll never forget that I muffed the first ball hit to me in my big league career.

I can't say it didn't bother me to make that error. Of course it did. I take pride in my fielding and, even though it turned out to be harmless, I had given the Phillies an extra out by dropping the ball. But anyone who plays baseball knows he's going to make mistakes once in a while. All you can do is put it behind you and get on with the game. It's one game in a long season and one misplay doesn't make or break it. I forgot about it on the next play. And I didn't think about it after the game was over.

In the third inning, I got my first major league hit, a single off of Floyd Youmans that drove in the first Cub run of the year and put us ahead, 1-0. It felt good to have that first hit under my belt. The guys had told me that Youmans throws hard, but I am always looking fastball and then I try to adjust to a curve or slider. The game stayed close all the way. We scored five runs on 12 hits, including two by Joe Girardi, starting in place of Damon Berryhill who was out with a sore arm. The paper said that Joe was the first rookie catcher to start on Opening Day for the Cubs since Randy Hundley in 1966. Joe's a good ballplayer and he did a great job. Mike Schmidt and Darren Daulton homered for the Phillies and Andre hit one for the Cubs and we took a 5-4 lead into the top of the ninth.

Looking back, maybe it was a sign of the kind of season we were going to have when Mitch Williams walked the bases loaded with nobody out. Everybody had heard that Mitch threw hard, had an unorthodox follow-through, and a tendency to be wild. Some of the fans were yelling "Goose" at him, remembering how unhappy they had been with Gossage as the closer last season. But then Mitch proceeded to strike out Chris James and the crowd cheered. Next was Mike Schmidt and everybody knows Schmidt's history against the Cubs. The park was a sea of noise when Schmidt, too, struck out. Now the fans were on their feet, almost not believing what they were seeing when Mitch fanned Mark Ryal to end the game. I had never seen anything like that in my whole life. What an introduction to major league baseball! Mitch is a character. He stays loose. I liked what he told the reporter who asked him how he expected to replace Palmeiro. He said, "I don't; I'm not an outfielder." But he *is* a pitcher.

After the game I met my family and we spent the evening talking about what a great day it had been.

April 5-6

In baseball you need to take the highs and the lows calmly, without letting yourself get too up or too down. Otherwise you'll be riding an emotional roller-coaster and losing your concentration. Opening Day was terrific, but the next day the Phillies beat us, 12-4. Ken Howell pitched for them and he really throws hard. Combine that with the fact that he threw five wild pitches and you get a sense of why most hitters don't like batting against him. I got one of our seven hits, but they scored seven runs in the fourth and ran away with it. When you get beat like that, you just go over it to see what mistakes you made and what you need to correct and then you just file it away in the past and get ready for the next game.

Unfortunately, the next day we ran into Steve Ontiveros and managed only five hits, including my first major league home run. Meanwhile, the Phillies got 15 hits and eight runs. It felt good to get that home run. I don't try to hit it out, but I'm strong enough that if I hit it right, it will reach the stands. I lift weights in the off-season and I work on strengthening my legs, arms, and wrists. But I don't lift during the season; I figure that then I am maintaining strength and tone by doing my regular exercizes every day. I'm always going to be more of a line drive hitter than a power hitter, but I'll still get my share of doubles and triples. I'm very content to bat first and not fourth in the lineup.

April 7-8-9

The next visitors to Wrigley were the Pittsburgh Pirates, who had been picked by most people to be a top contender. They've got some good ballplayers, guys like Bonilla, LaValliere, Bonds, Van Slyke, Drabek, and Walk. In the first game of the series, we beat them, 6-5. It was a good game. We scored four in the second inning, in which I had a two-run double. They then scored three in the fourth and two in the sixth to go up, 5-4. Andre and Mark drove in runs in the bottom of the sixth and Mitch came in to save the game for Steve Wilson. We were starting to get our rhythm as a team and the next day we took the Pirates again behind Mike Bielecki, 5-3. Domingo Ramos—replacing Shawon Dunston who was out with an injury—hit a two-run homer and the next day went 3-for-3 with two RBIs, as we finished the sweep of the Pirates with an 8-3 win. Rick Sutcliffe and I got consecutive bunt hits, so everybody started getting on Rick about his speed. I've been on teams where some guys don't get along with others, but from the very beginning this team got along well and had fun together. I come back to that again and again because, if there was anything that kept us on an even keel when we were on winning or losing streaks, it was our ability to kid each other and have a good time together.

April 11-12

We closed our first home stand with two straight wins over the Cardinals, giving us a 6-2 start. In the first game against the Cardinals, I led off with a home run off of Jose DeLeon. He throws hard. I mean he *slings* the ball. When you're facing a fastballer like DeLeon, Dibble, Howell, or Gooden, you can't let yourself be afraid. But it's okay to hope that he doesn't hit you. I step toward the plate from my open stance, so I'm used to being brushed back. But I don't like anybody throwing at me intentionally any more than they would like me bunting down the first-base line so that I could give them a message when they come over to pick up the ball.

I scared myself because I usually don't hit home runs early. I get two or three in the middle of a season and that's it. Here I was with two homers in seven games. That hit gave me at least one hit in each of our first seven games. That was important to me because I felt like I was contributing to the team and, as a leadoff man, I'm supposed to get the offense going every time I come up, not just in the first inning. It was nice to hit that homer, but it was even better to score the winning run on a groundout in the eighth. The Cardinals have some great players: Brunansky has a strong arm; Coleman is a great baserunner; Guerrero is a hitter; and Ozzie Smith is in a class by himself. I was hitless in the second game against the Cardinals, but we won, 3-2, behind Paul Kilgus and Mitch, who came in to get the last out.

It was time to pack up and get ready for my first road trip. When you're going on the road, you can drive out to the airport yourself or go to Wrigley and take the bus to O'Hare with the Cubs people. On the first couple of trips I took the bus. I was looking forward to playing in stadiums around the league and to seeing the other major league cities. But I was also looking forward to the meal money. For the 10-day road trip, the meal money was $600. Rick Sutcliffe was laughing when Peter Durso, our traveling secretary, handed out the envelopes. He said, "Hey, Juice, this was a whole month's pay when you were in Double-A." And he was right. To a rookie, the meal money is great because I don't see how anybody can eat $60-worth of food in a day. Of course, I once had a hamburger and a coke in a fancy hotel and it cost $18.00. So I guess if you wanted to eat like that, you could spend it all. I developed a routine where, if it was a night game, I'd eat something about one in the afternoon and then later I'd have a sandwich in the clubhouse.

When we travel we wear sportcoats and slacks. There is no drinking on the plane. Once we're in town, we can dress any way we want. After the game, if there's a nice club or something, some of us might go there and listen to the music and hang out. I usually don't stay up late because I need to be rested to play well. First and second-year players have to have roommates on the road. Peter Durso tries to match people who are friends. My first roomie was Rick Wrona, then I roomed with Dwight Smith when he was called up from Iowa.

I can see that road trips can be a real temptation to big league players. You are staying in the best hotels, you are a celebrity because you play in the major leagues, you are recognized and sought after and, if you have a particularly good game, you might have a few drinks to celebrate it or, if you have a bad one, a few drinks to forget it. I've never had a desire to drink or to use any substance that is an artificial way of altering moods. It's okay if somebody wants to have a drink, but I have no tolerance at all for anyone who risks life by driving under the influence. And I think drugs are the worst thing you can do to yourself. I wish everyone could find something that they were good at and really enjoyed doing so they could feel good about themselves. Baseball does that for me.

April 14-15-16

Veterans Stadium in Philadelphia is a nice park, except for the fact that it has artificial turf. This was the first time I had ever played on it and, even though it is supposed to give the advantage to players with good speed, I really don't like it. It's tough on the legs, the bounces are crazy, and it's just not as much fun as grass.

I went hitless in the game on Friday, but we won, 6-4, behind Scott Sanderson and Mitch. Andre doubled in two runs in the first and Joe Girardi drove home a run in the second and we were on our way. Everyone was feeling good because we were off to the kind of start that nobody—except us—thought we could have.

On Saturday it rained all day. Nobody likes a rainout because it means somewhere down the road you'll have to play a doubleheader and it might come at a time when your pitching is tired or your hitting is off. You'd rather play now. I spent the day doing some shopping and taking it easy.

On Sunday we beat the Phillies again, 5-3, and Rick won his third game. He drove in two runs with a single and he seemed happier about that than anything. He's a good hitter for a pitcher. Maybe 10 years from now he'll be a designated hitter in the American League.

This was my third straight game without a hit. That brought out one of the differences you find in the major leagues. In the minors, if you're going badly for a while, guys come by and pep you up and get you going. I started off in the majors with hits in my first seven games and then I dropped off a little. I didn't have many guys come up to me and tell me that it was going to be okay. I mean I figure that I can take care of my hitting, but it doesn't hurt to have somebody who has been in the big leagues for a while let you know that he's on your side and that he thinks you belong at this level. The guy who made a point of encouraging me was Shawon Dunston. Even though he himself wasn't off to a real good start, he made it a point to tell me, "Don't worry about it, just keep going." I think that's more important to the rookies than to anyone else. Once you've been in the majors for a while, you know you belong and you really don't need anyone to reassure you. And that's different from talking to someone whose error lost a game. Errors are part of the game and it's understood that no one has to come up to a player and say, "Forget it." What I learned from all that is that next year and down the road I'll remember to say an encouraging word to our rookies when it looks like it might help.

I mentioned earlier that the big difference between the pitching in the minors and the majors is the command that the pitchers up here have over their stuff. But there is another, less obvious, advantage that major league pitchers enjoy and that is the scouting reports. Minor league teams can't afford to send advance scouts to study the teams that are next on the schedule. In the majors, advance scouts chart how the batters are faring against different kinds of pitching, where the fielders are playing them, who is running well and who isn't, and so forth. They are particularly anxious to observe the rookies or newcomers to the league. If a player has a consistent batting weakness, the scouts will spot it and, when their team plays you, their pitchers will try to exploit

it. Word travels fast. The hitters who can't adjust
their mechanics won't be around very long.

Then, too, it works both ways. Our scouts report
on their pitchers and on any special situation, such
as a fielder with a sore arm, that will enable us to take
an extra base if the situation allows. Teammates help
rookies by telling them what to look for from particular pitchers. And, finally, with every at-bat you build
your own memory bank of what a pitcher threw you
and what you did right or wrong with it.

It is important for a ballplayer to remember that,
even in the midst of a hitting slump, he needs to do
everything he can to help his team win. If you let your
last at-bat distract you while you are in the field, it
can lead to a loss of concentration and costly defensive mistakes.

We left for Montreal with a seven-game winning
streak and a record of 8-2. It is nice to put together
a string of wins anytime, but it means even more
when you do it right at the start of the season. Then,
if you lose a few in a row, you know you're capable not
only of breaking a losing streak but of putting a series
of wins together again.

April 17-18-19

I can't say that I like Olympic Stadium in Montreal. There is something about the lights and the
background that makes it tough to see the ball. We
lost the series opener, 2-1, as Kevin Gross bested
Greg Maddux. I had a single and got hit by a pitch,
but we stranded 10 runners and lost. We lost again
the next night, 11-2. I had a double in four trips, but
it just wasn't our night. Then the Expos completed
the sweep with a 3-2 win, despite the fact that we out-
hit them 9 to 4. I had another double, but that's all

in five trips. We weren't losing because we were trying too hard or pressing. We could have won two of those three games; we just didn't get it done. The Expos looked like a very good team; they have pitching and some tough hitters like Hubie Brooks, Tim Raines, and Andres Callaraga. But I think, position for position, we're better.

April 20-21-23

We moved on to New York for a four-game series against the Mets. Shea Stadium is a great place to play—a nice ball park, good visibility, and natural turf. I was anxious to see the Mets, since all of the experts had picked them to win the division. They proceeded to beat us three out of four.

In game one, I faced Doc Gooden for the first time and I realized that if everybody pitched the way he does, a lot of hitters would be looking for work. I guess his fastball isn't as fast as it used to be, but when you mix it with his changeup, breaking balls, and excellent control, he is some pitcher. We got three runs off of him, but for the first time Mitch couldn't hold the lead and the Mets scored twice in the seventh for a 4-3 win. I was 0-for-4 and three for my last 16 times at bat. But I was making good contact and I felt it was just a matter of time until hits would start coming.

We won the second game of the series as Rick Sutcliffe, with help from Steve Wilson, earned his fourth straight, 8-4. I was glad to be able to contribute two doubles and score two runs. Mitch Webster had three hits and Ryno had two, helping make up for the fact that Sut went hitless in three trips.

In the Saturday game, Greg Maddux lost another tough one, 3-1. He'd pitched well enough to have a 2-1 record instead of 0-3. Sid Fernandez and Roger McDowell were tough, particularly Fernandez, who uses his size to hide the ball and disguise his change of speed.

On Sunday we lost for the sixth time on our seven-game road trip, 4-2, to Rick Aguilera of the Mets, who won in relief of Ron Darling. Andre homered for us and it was the 300th of his career, but we couldn't get a rally going and we saw our record slip from 8-2 to 9-8 on one road trip. But no one else in the division was winning consistently, so we came back to Chicago in a first-place tie with Montreal and Philadelphia. We had played the Mets tough, even if we did lose three of four, and, in spite of all their publicity, they didn't look unbeatable.

April 25-26-27

Homecoming didn't start out real well. We got shut out by Tim Belcher of the Dodgers, 4-0, on five hits on April 25 and then on Wednesday Mike Morgan beat us with relief help from Jay Howell, 3-1. Rick gave up only three runs in eight innings, but they all came in the third and we just weren't able to string our eight hits together and score some runs. The next day turned things around for us. Greg Maddux and Orel Hershiser both pitched great ball. I had to leave the game in the fourth inning when I pulled the hamstring in my right leg. It didn't seem serious at the time, but it hurt enough to slow me down and I couldn't play on it. I think it actually got weakened in Montreal. Playing on artificial turf is different than playing on grass and, if you're running at full speed on turf, I think it's tougher on your legs and muscles.

Gary Varsho took my place and made a diving catch on Mike Scioscia's drive with the bases loaded in the fourth. Then, in the fifth, Gary hit a triple to right, driving in Maddux with the only run of the game. It was a great game to win, especially beating the defending World Champions and their best pitcher.

Early in the season, I developed a daily routine for game days in Chicago. I normally get up about 8:30 and most of the time I don't eat breakfast. I leave for the park about 9:30. Usually there are a few dozen people standing by the fence outside Wrigley where the players park their cars. The players say hello but there really isn't time to sign autographs. All starters have to be dressed by 10:55, so you usually want to be in the dressing room by 10:00 or earlier if you have an injury that needs treatment by the trainer.

I stretch my muscles before I go out for batting practice. The batting practice pitchers are coaches on the team and they throw pretty well. I use the practice to aim at spots, work on bunting, or whatever I think I need that day. After my turn in the cage, I go to the outfield and shag flies, check the wind, and loosen up my arm. Batting practice ends about noon and we go back into the clubhouse. There is a sandwich and soft drink spread there and usually I eat something and then sign some baseballs, read, and answer fan mail, watch TV, or whatever. This year a lot of my mail has been from kids sending my rookie card and asking me to sign it or asking for an autographed picture. The Cubs give us a big supply of photographs to use for these. I also get letters from various charities wanting an appearance or a donation and regular fan letters and occasionally a few from ladies who say they'd like to meet me.

Normally reporters are allowed in the clubhouse for 15 minutes or so right after batting practice. They come back after the game and go to Zim's office first and then come into the clubhouse to talk with the players about the game. I don't go off in a corner and psych myself up before a game. I move around the clubhouse, answer my fan mail, and wait until it's time to go back on the field.

After a game, when I'm dressed and go out to my car, I usually take some time to sign autographs for a while or give out signed pictures. The fans are really nice and they always say thanks.

Then I usually drive home to my apartment and later I cook something up for dinner and watch the tape of my at-bats during the game. These are the tapes shot by Bob Sears from the dugout. I asked him to give me a tape of all my at-bats and every night I take it home and study it—sometimes over and over until I see what I'm doing—or not doing.

When I started to slump a bit, I looked at my Peoria tape first to study my approach to the ball. Then I watched the most recent game when I wasn't hitting well. I would then run the tape back to where I had some good at-bats up here to see how I was doing the same things that I was doing in Peoria. I could see what I was doing wrong. Mostly I was studying where my feet were and how my hands were going through the zone. Usually what the tapes tell me is that I need to make a minor adjustment. Sometimes I go over one at-bat about 15 times if I have to. If you want to stay in the game, you need to dedicate yourself to that kind of work. Bob Sears gave me three tapes that have my at-bats through the whole season so that I can study them over the winter.

April 28-29-30

After the Dodgers, the Padres came to Wrigley to meet us. I had heard a lot about the Padres and read that they were favored to win the Western Division. Paul Kilgus pitched really well against them in the first game that Friday. He had the luxury of a three-run lead in the first, thanks to Ryno's home run and an RBI single by Darrin Jackson. The Padres didn't even get a hit until Randy Ready singled with two out in the sixth.But in the ninth they threatened when they scored once and had runners on first and second with two outs. Zim called Mitch in from the pen and he saved the game without throwing a pitch. All he did was to whirl and pick Carmelo Martinez, a former Cub, off second to end the game. We won, 3-1.

The Padres got us back the next day in what has to be described as an ugly game. There were 11 errors and we had five of them. How many times will Ryne Sandberg ever commit two errors in one game? Mike Bielecki struck out 10 Padres, but we still managed to lose, 5-4. Games like this are better forgotten.

We ended April with a win, 7-3, over San Diego. Scott Sanderson pitched seven good innings for us and we got 10 hits, most of them early off Eric Show, to sew up the win.

We left Chicago for the West Coast. I was looking forward to seeing great cities like San Francisco, Los Angeles, and San Diego. Even more, I was looking forward to an end to the bothersome hamstring pain and a chance to play again after missing the last three games.

So we finished April in fourth place; it was really too early to say what might lie ahead.

National League East Standings				
April 30, 1989				
	W	**L**	**Pct.**	**GB**
St. Louis	13	9	.591	—
New York	12	10	.545	1
Montreal	13	11	.542	1
CHICAGO	12	11	.522	$1^{1/2}$
Philadelphia	11	12	.478	$2^{1/2}$
Pittsburgh	10	14	.417	4

 **Hanging Tough**

May started with good news. Damon Berryhill was reinstated to the active list and Dwight Smith was recalled from Iowa. It wasn't good news though for Joe Girardi and Phil Stephenson, since they were sent to Iowa to make room on the roster for Damon and Dwight. We knew that Joe would back because he's a good catcher and Phil was a better hitter than he had shown in his three weeks of part-time play.

Damon is recognized as one of the best catchers in the league and Dwight had a .325 batting average at Iowa in 21 games and 12 of his 27 hits were for extra bases.

May 1-2

We opened the month of May against the Giants in San Francisco. Most of the time their stadium is a fielder's nightmare. They can talk all they want about the winds at Wrigley, but nothing I've ever seen before or since compares to my first experience of Candlestick Park. I was still hobbled with my ham-

51

string injury, but I was in the outfield before the game shagging flies and testing the flight of the balls. I couldn't believe what I saw. A couple of balls that were headed toward the outfield got caught in the wind and simply fell straight down! Even guys who have played with the Giants for years can't always read the winds or the particular swirl they cause.

Damon was the hero of our first meeting with the Giants when he homered in the top of the 12th and Calvin Schiraldi shut them down in the bottom of the inning, striking out two, to save the win for Jeff Pico, 4-3.

It was good we won that one because the next night we came up against Rick Reuschel. Dwight played left and got his first two major league hits; Damon added two and Ryno three to the team total of 11, but we still couldn't score and lost, 4-0.

May 3-4

Then it was on to Jack Murphy Stadium in San Diego. The Padres have a good team and lots of people picked them to win the Western Division. The stadium is nice and San Diego is a great city. More importantly, we took both games from the Padres. The first one will be remembered by anyone who watched it on TV. We were tied, 3-3, in the sixth when Andre, who had homered earlier, blasted a triple scoring Ryno and then Mark followed with a hit to drive in Andre. The Padres scored one in the bottom of the sixth and it stayed 5-4 into the bottom of the ninth. The Padres had Flannery on second base with one out and Mitch struck out Tony Gwynn. Then he got Jack Clark to hit a grounder toward the hole at short. Shawon came up with it and fired. Mark Grace made an incredible catch of what would have been a wild throw to tie the game. It was a little scary, but it was a good win.

We got another "W" the next day when Mike Bielecki threw his first major league shutout, a five-hit, 4-0 game that lifted our season record to 15-12. Andre was hot. He had four hits, including back-to-back triples. It seemed like he was really relaxed, just going up there and doing his thing. He told Dwight and me that we'd be able to tell when he was really in a hot streak because he'd have a game in which he'd hit two homers.

May 5-6-7

After sweeping the two games from San Diego, we moved into Los Angeles for three. Dodger Stadium is really first class. It's always exciting because the crowds are always big and there are celebrities everywhere. You see people on the field during the pre-game workouts and you recognize them from TV or the movies.

We won the opener, 4-2, behind Scott Sanderson and Mitch. But the real hero of the game was Andre, who had four hits, giving him a string of eight straight hits. Two of his hits in this game were homers, as if he needed to prove that he was hot!

Mike Morgan and Jay Howell shut us out the next day, 3-0, and when Andre lined to right in the first, his string was over. He got one hit later in the game, but it didn't matter. It was just one of those games when we couldn't get any offense going.

On Sunday, we came back to beat the Dodgers, 4-2, and it was the second time we made a loser out of Hershiser. It was Damon's two-run single with the bases loaded in the sixth that put us ahead to stay. It was an exciting win and we were ready to go home to Wrigley, tied for first with the Mets.

On the plane coming back, I could tell that Andre

was having a lot of trouble with his right knee. He was in a lot of pain and it was the same knee that had to be drained of fluid about three weeks earlier. We had the day off on Monday and then the Giants were in town for two games. We learned that Andre was going on the 21-day disabled list, retroactive to May 7, and that he was going to have arthroscopic surgery on his knee. Anytime you lose a starter, it's a bad deal. But when you lose an Andre Dawson, it's worse than that. He is a great player and a leader and you feel better when he's in there with you.

May 9

I think the team mood might have been down a little, but whatever it was, we lost to the Giants, 4-2, on two unearned runs. We needed to score some runs and prove that we could stay in the race until we got Andre back. I know that was in the back of my mind when I said I was ready to play on Wednesday against the Giants. My hamstring was still a little sore, but I really was feeling good and I wanted to play.

May 10

On Wednesday night, we were losing, 4-3, in the ninth inning and I was the tying run on first. Domingo Ramos singled to left. Mitchell was playing fairly deep and I thought the ball would slow down in the grass before it got to him so that I could beat his throw to third. That way I'd be in a position to score on a wild pitch, a balk, or whatever. I turned it on full speed and, as I came off second base, I heard a "pop" in my leg and I felt like someone had shot me. My leg just gave out on me and I went down face first. I couldn't move. I was lying there beating the dirt with my fist because of the pain while I got tagged out. I had never experienced any pain like that before. A couple of teammates helped me off the field and I went to the training room. To make matters worse, we lost the game, 4-3.

The doctor was in the training room at the time, so he checked the muscle over and he couldn't feel that it was torn. His preliminary diagnosis was that I had pulled it again. It turned out later that the reason he couldn't recognize it as torn was because it was such a deep tear. The hamstrings are the muscles you use to move your hips and knees, so it was serious business.

Later, the pain was so bad that I had to go to the hospital. I wanted to see Doctor Schafer, but the irony was that he was in surgery operating on Andre's knee. They gave me some painkillers and told me to come back the next day for more testing.

The next day, they put me in one of those large machines that move you back and forth and use sound waves and other hi-tech methods to find out what is wrong. At that point it was clear that there was a deep longitudinal tear in my right hamstring. We had that Thursday off—the day I found out the hamstring was torn and that I wasn't going to be able to play again for a long time. The Cubs put me on the 15-day disabled list and called up Doug Dascenzo from Iowa, only two days after they had recalled Phil Stephenson to take Andre's place on the roster.

It's tough to go down with an injury anytime. But to be a rookie in the big leagues and in the process of getting used to playing at that level, having a serious injury is one tough experience. It isn't that you don't think you'll recover. It is more a matter of feeling that your rhythm and that of the team is thrown-off, particularly in light of the fact that only a few days earlier we had lost our gold glove in right field and one of our main hitters—Andre Dawson. If ever you're going to get down, that might be a time to do it. I called home and it really helped to talk to my mom and Jonathan and Tammy. They are people I don't want to let down and I knew that I'd do whatever it took to get back to full strength.

The doctor and trainer put me on a routine to repair the tear and build the muscle back up. Mainly I used the whirlpool, rode the exercise bike, and did leg lifts. It was monotonous and frustrating because I wanted to be playing, but I got a real lift when some of the guys came by and said, "Hurry up and get well. You're doing all right and we need you back in the lineup." That kind of gets you to the point where you want to work, work, and work—to do anything that would speed up the time it takes to make it right again. I can't even begin to describe how much it meant to me to know that the team wanted me back out there and that Zim let me know that the job was mine when I was ready.

May 12

At this point, we were missing our starting catcher and two-thirds of our outfield and we went into the first of three games with Houston just two games above .500. Jim Deschaies shut us down on four hits and the only run we could score was on a steal of home by Darrin Jackson in the sixth. We lost, 3-1; even so, our guys weren't giving up—they were just trying to hold until we were back at full strength.

May 13

Houston beat us again, this time, 1-0. Greg Maddux pitched a three-hitter, but so did Knepper and Smith for the Astros and they managed to put two doubles together in the eighth to score a run. You could tell that this was a game we knew we should have won. Nobody said anything, but you could sense it. Greg must have been wondering what he had to do to win, but you never sensed that he was mad or sad or blamed his teammates.

May 14

One of the last pitchers you want to face when you are in a losing streak and having trouble scoring runs is Mike Scott of the Astros. He beat us, 5-1, and allowed only four hits and even our one run wasn't earned. This was our fifth straight loss at home, starting when Andre went down.

People began saying that the Cubs wouldn't win without Andre in there, much less with any other starters out as well. Some of the writers began to highlight the fact that the Cubs had scored only seven runs in the five-game homestand and that this would be a long year for Cub fans. To make matters worse, Mitch Webster injured his leg and joined Andre and me on the disabled list that same day. Things just didn't look good. The Cubs called up Lloyd McClendon from Iowa where he was hitting .321. Although Lloyd had been up with the Cincinnati Reds in 1987 for 45 games and in 1988 for 72 games as an infielder-catcher, this was the break he needed to show what he could do. Lloyd is a good player and a tough competitor. Except for his time up with the Reds, he had spent eight years in the minors. He had paid his dues. He was ready.

May 15

Was he ever ready! Lloyd's first game as a Cub is the kind they put in the movies. Here we were in the middle of a losing streak at home, one game under

.500, with our starting outfield on the disabled list. Lloyd came up for his first at-bat in a Cub uniform with two men on in the second inning and proceeded to hit a three-run homer against Derek Lilliquist of the Braves. It didn't just put us ahead in the game, which we went on to win, 4-0, behind Mike Bielecki. It was like a shot of adrenalin to the whole team. I think it just woke us up and reminded us that, even without some of our starters, we could hang in there and win. Lloyd didn't have a lot of major league experience, but he was a seasoned pro and he showed right away that he could play. That was a game—and a boxscore—to remember.

Cubs 4, Braves 0									
	ab	r	h	bi		ab	r	h	bi
Gant 3b	4	0	0	0	Dascenzo cf	4	0	0	0
Acker p	0	0	0	0	Ramos ss	4	0	2	1
Blocker ph	1	0	0	0	Sandberg 2b	4	0	0	0
L. Smith lf	4	0	0	0	Grace 1b	4	1	1	0
Evans 1b	4	0	0	0	Berryhill c	3	1	1	0
D. Murphy cf	4	0	2	0	McClendon lf	3	1	2	3
Thomas ss	4	0	0	0	Wilkerson 3b	3	0	0	0
D. James rf	3	0	2	0	Jackson rf	2	1	1	0
J. Davis c	4	0	0	0	Bielecki p	1	0	0	0
Tredway 2b	3	0	1	0	Stephenson ph	1	0	0	0
Lilliquist p	2	0	1	0	Schiraldi p	0	0	0	0
G. Perry 1b	1	0	1	0					
Totals	**34**	**0**	**7**	**0**	**Totals**	**29**	**4**	**7**	**4**

Atlanta	000	000	000—0	
CUBS	030	010	00x—4	

E—D. Murphy, Ramos. DP—Atlanta 1, CUBS 1. LOB—Atlanta 10, CUBS 3. 2B—D. Murphy, D. James. HR—McClendon (1). S—Bielecki.

	IP	H	R	ER	BB	SO
Atlanta						
Lilliquist L, 2-3	6	6	4	4	1	2
Acker	2	1	0	0	0	1
CUBS						
Bielecki W, 3-1	7	4	0	0	3	1
Schiraldi	2	3	0	0	0	2

Umpires—Home, Bonin; First, Harvey; Second, Pulli; Third, Davidson.
T—2:04 A—16,920.

May 16

Almost as though the sound of Lloyd's bat woke us up, we came out of a slump. We didn't waste any time going after Tom Glavine of the Braves in the second game of the series. Ryno's two-run triple, followed by a single by Mark, brought home three of the four runs we scored in the first inning. That's all we got all day, but with Scott Sanderson and Mitch pitching, that's all we needed. We won, 4-3, as Mitch got his 11th save in our total of 19 wins.

May 17

We did it again—scored four runs early—and beat the Braves, 4-0, behind Jeff Pico, who started in place of Rick. He was having back spasms and Dick Pole and Zim figured it was best to sit him down for a turn. Even though it might have looked like we were headed toward having trouble finding nine guys to put out on the field, the team was getting used to pulling together and it was exciting to see who would provide the spark on any given day.

May 18

I stayed home and rested instead of going to the charity exhibition game between the Cubs and White Sox at Comiskey Park. It's called the Windy City Classic and it drew the largest crowd Comiskey Park had all year, 35,522. I don't know how much of a classic it was because we made four errors and the White Sox made two and they won the game, 5-4.

May 19

Back to business and a six-game road trip. Riverfront Stadium, except for the artificial turf, is a great place to play. You see the ball well both at the plate and in the field. And it's a nice city to visit with its many really good restaurants along the river.

Something else that is nice is the fact that there are a lot of Cub fans in the Cincinnati area and we can always count on a great deal of support when we play there.

Once again we scored early with four in the fourth and three more in the fifth while Greg was holding the Reds to six hits and two runs. We coasted in, 8-2. It was extra fun because Zim won an argument with the umpires on a batted ball that hit Ryno and that helped us keep the rally going in the fourth. We kidded Zim about getting kicked out of the game; but he won his point and that's not something you see every day. Neither is the double steal pulled off by Damon and Lloyd, with Lloyd stealing home.

May 20

This was Lloyd McClendon's day as he got us off to a good start with a homer in the second inning and we went on to a 7-3 win, after scoring six runs in the first four innings. Paul Kilgus got the win with help from Pat Perry, who hadn't allowed a run in his last 19 innings.

I hated sitting on the bench. I mean it was great being part of the team but I wanted to be out there doing my part. All I could do was keep working on healing and strengthening my leg and cheer for the guys who were out there playing hard every day. Zim had been using Doug Dascenzo, Dwight Smith, Darrin Jackson, and Gary Varsho in the outfield and, the way Lloyd had been hitting, Zim was going to play him in the outfield as well as at third, first, or catcher as needed. Even though he had never played out there, I think that with work he could develop into a good outfielder. He's a good hitter and a dedicated ballplayer.

May 21

Our five-game winning streak came to an end as the Reds beat us, 7-2. Rick Mahler held us scoreless in every inning but the sixth, while Mike Bielecki and Jeff Pico got roughed up by the Reds. It was kind of a bad day all the way around. Zim brought Mitch in to get some work and in two innings he walked three, hit two, gave up two hits, picked a runner off, threw a wild pitch, and committed a balk. You knew it was Mitch's year when all that happened and they only scored one run off of him. This was a game to forget even before we got on the plane for Houston.

May 22

I don't like the Astrodome, especially on defense. It doesn't get completely dark in Houston until late and the light coming through the roof makes it hard to track flyballs.

We beat the Astros, 5-3, and moved into a first-place tie with the Mets. This was Rick's first start in 10 days and he shut out the Astros through seven innings. In the eighth they scored three runs before Calvin Schiraldi shut them down. I was especially happy because my roommate and good friend Dwight came through with a pinch-hit triple to clear the bases in the fifth.

Dwight is a great ballplayer. We agreed in spring training that we were going to be number one and number two in the voting for Rookie of the Year and that, whoever got it, it would be okay with the other. When he got sent to Iowa before the season, we both knew he'd be back up before long. Now here he was really pitching in and helping to carry the team. I think Dwight will be a .300 hitter in his major league career and that he is going to develop into a good outfielder. He has a great deal of speed and a strong arm. Just as important, he doesn't let anything bother him. He doesn't put pressure on himself. He's crazy; he loves to have fun and make people laugh and there's no doubt in my mind that he really helped keep the team loose all season.

We're like brothers; I can talk to Dwight about anything and trust that it stays between us. We respect each other and we enjoy being together. It saves money, too, because I don't have to buy any music, all I have to do is listen to Dwight sing.

We talk baseball a lot and all season we just kept telling each other that, "Hey, we're in the big leagues and we're in first place, and can you believe it?" After that Monday's game when we were back in the room, Dwight got that big smile on his face and said, "Oh, man, can I hit?!" and we both laughed.

May 23

We claimed sole possession of first place by beating the Astros, 5-4. Dwight, Mark, and Gary Varsho each had two hits and we scored five runs in five-and-two-thirds innings off of Mike Scott who, whether he scuffs it or not, is one of the best pitchers in baseball. Houston rallied for four runs in the sixth, but then Pat Perry and Calvin Schiraldi came on in relief of Scott Sanderson and closed them down the rest of the way.

Lots of people thought that we would sink when the injuries hit us. But we didn't think so and the longer we played well while Zim was juggling his lineups and getting the best out of everyone he had, the more we felt we'd stay in the race all the way when we were all healthy again.

May 24

Shawon had the clutch hit again as we completed the sweep in Houston with a 3-1 win. His single with two outs in the fourth scored Damon and Lloyd and gave Greg all he needed to get the win and left us two full games ahead of the division. Winning in the Astrodome is great; sweeping in the Astrodome is magnificent; flying home to Chicago in first place is just plain fun. And we had a day off to enjoy it.

May 26

Maybe Rolando Roomes wanted to take a page out of Lloyd's book, I don't know. But he went 3-for-6, including the two-run homer in the 12th inning that beat us, 10-8. Rolando had surprised the fans, and maybe even Pete Rose, with his hitting and hustle. But those of us who knew him in the minors knew that he could play the game. And you respect somebody who works hard to get a chance and then makes the best of it. The Roomes for McClendon trade was the best kind because it helped both players and both teams.

It was a very tough game to lose. We were ahead, 7-2, at the end of six and then had to come back to score one in the bottom of the ninth to tie it at eight and send it into extra innings. Rob Dibble came on for the Reds to pitch the last two innings and he struck out five of the six hitters he retired in order. He may be the fastest pitcher in the league. In the locker room, you could tell we knew we should have won, but we didn't and all we could do about it was come back tomorrow.

May 27

My 14 days on the disabled list were up but I still wasn't ready to play so the Cubs moved me to the 21-day D.L. All I could do at that point was hope that my recovery continued and that I'd be able to come back in a week. We kept our one-and-a-half-game hold on first place on Saturday by beating the Reds, 5-3, behind Rick's four-hit pitching. We scored two in the first and two more in the third and Sut stole a base in the process. The only negative was that Ryno was hit by a Jose Rijo pitch and had to leave the game. Fortunately, it wasn't a serious injury. Vance Law had two hits and three RBIs yesterday and an RBI single today. He's a really good guy who knows how to kid around; but when he's on the field, he's all business. He was going through kind of a tough year, but he belonged in there and gave it all he had. It was good to come back from the disappointing loss of the day before and the clubhouse was a happy place when the reporters came in after the game. Dwight was 2-for-2 with two RBIs, so you knew he'd be smiling.

May 28

Mike Bielecki kept us on the right track by holding the Reds to one run on seven hits while we scored six times on 11. Dwight came up as a pinch hitter in the seventh and drove home a double and now he'd hit safely in seven straight games. But it was our three-run rally in the sixth, two coming home on Shawon's single, that iced it for us. It was a short homestand and now we were off to Atlanta and St. Louis for six games.

May 29

Here we were in Atlanta—35 miles from my hometown—and I wasn't able to play. But I went out to the outfield during batting practice and I experienced at least a little of the thrill of being on the field in the stadium that I had seen so often on television while growing up.

The Braves beat us on a good job by rookie pitcher Derek Lilliquist, 2-1. Sanderson pitched really well for us, allowing only three hits and two runs in six innings, but we could only get one run in the seventh when we had the chance to score more. Those are the kind of things that haunt you a little after a loss like that, yet you have to put the game behind you and come through better tomorrow.

I like being in Atlanta because it gives me a chance to visit with my family and friends from Newnan. My son Jonathan is getting big; I wish he was with me all the time but I stay as close to him as I can and I'll be able to spend a lot of time with him during the off-season.

May 30

Mark Grace continued to be a leader for the Cubs. Today, he scored on Damon's double in the second, putting us ahead, 1-0. In the third he drove in Gary Varsho from third and in the fifth he singled to drive in Doug Dascenzo with what proved to be the winning run, as we edged the Braves, 3-2. Greg pitched another strong game and Mitch came on to get his 13th save. Mitch Webster came off the disabled list; one back, two to come.

May 31

We ran into some bad luck the next day. Most of it was in the person of John Smoltz, who got his seventh win by beating us, 3-2. The Braves scored the winning run in the sixth when Shawon made a throwing error, but those things happen in baseball and we had other opportunities to get some runs but we couldn't take advantage of them. Even so, as May ended we were still in first place. A couple of writers were already starting to warn about something called a "June swoon," but that wasn't anything that this team knew about or feared.

National League East Standings				
May 31, 1989				
	W	L	Pct.	GB
CHICAGO	28	22	.560	—
Montreal	27	25	.519	2
New York	25	24	.510	$2^{1/2}$
St. Louis	23	25	.479	4
Pittsburgh	21	28	.429	$6^{1/2}$
Philadelphia	18	31	.367	9

Jerome Walton with a closed stance—senior year at Newnan High. *(Photo courtesy of the Newnan Times-Herald.)*

Jerome is welcomed by teammates after a home run for Newnan High School in the spring of his senior year. *(Photo courtesy of the Newnan Times-Herald.)*

Jerome went to spring training with a goal—to be Rookie of the Year. *(Photo courtesy of TV Sports Mailbag.)*

Determination and concentration are the trademarks of Jerome's approach to the game. *(Photo courtesy of the Chicago Cubs.)*

Eighteen bunt hits in 1989 mark Jerome as one of the top
bunters in baseball. *(Photo courtesy of the Chicago Cubs.)*

Juice led the Cubs with 24 stolen bases in 31 attempts in 1989. *(Photo courtesy of TV Sports Mailbag.)*

Jerome's wide open stance allows him to see and attack the ball. *(Photo courtesy of the Chicago Cubs.)*

Jerome's first major league home run came off of Steve Ontiveros of Philadelphia on April 6. Here he is congratulated by third base coach, Chuck Cottier, after homering later in the season at Wrigley. *(Photo courtesy of the Chicago Cubs.)*

Even a ground ball was dangerous with Walton up. He had 30 infield hits in 1989. *(Photo courtesy of the Chicago Cubs.)*

Jonathan Walton visits Dad in the dugout. *(Photo courtesy of the Chicago Cubs.)*

Juice scored 64 runs—third best on the 1989 Cubs.
(Photo courtesy of the Chicago Cubs.)

In 133 starts, Jerome opened games by reaching base 40
times. *(Photo courtesy of the Chicago Cubs.)*

Jerome's 30-game hitting streak set a modern Cub record.
(Photo courtesy of the Chicago Cubs.)

Speed and steadiness are the trademarks of Jerome's defensive work. *(Photo courtesy of the Chicago Cubs.)*

Juice makes difficult catches look routine. *(Photo courtesy of the Chicago Cubs.)*

The 1989 Chicago Cubs celebrate after clinching the National League Eastern Division title on September 26 in Montreal. For Jerome Walton, it was a memorable moment and a magical rookie year. *(Photo courtesy of the Chicago Cubs.)*

Jerome and best friend Dwight Smith were the first Cub teammates ever to finish 1-2 in the Rookie of the Year voting.
(Photo courtesy of the Chicago Cubs.)

Rookie mayor Richard M. Daley of Chicago (left) greets the
1989 National League Rookie of the Year and his attorney
Terry Sullivan (right).

Juice tells Santa that he wants a World Championship ring in 1990. *(Photo courtesy of the Chicago Cubs.)*

No Swoon
This June

June 2

After a day off, we moved into St. Louis for three games. It was a wild scene. There were thousands of Cub fans there and it was almost like what a World Series atmosphere must be like. The fans in St. Louis are wild. Busch Stadium is a really nice ball park; the only thing that would make it better is natural grass.

Rick got his seventh win of the year in 10 decisions and we beat the Cardinals, 5-2. Lloyd had three hits and Shawon had a run-producing triple. We led all the way and the Cards didn't score until the eighth and then Zim brought in Mitch to shut down the rally. In the afternoon, Mitch had visited the National Bowling Hall of Fame and rolled some frames while he was there. Everybody wanted to know how his control was. Well, it was good enough that night! We knew that the Cardinals would be in the race and that made beating them in their home park extra fun. Although we were playing our games one at a time, we knew that this game began a stretch where we would play our next 17 games against St. Louis, the Mets, and Montreal. So the next two-and-a-half weeks looked to be exciting.

June 3

Dwight told me that he was seeing the ball real well lately and he proved it on this day with a bases-loaded double that drove in three runs that put us ahead, 4-3, in the third inning. The Cardinals came back to take the lead in the sixth, 5-4, and it stayed that way until Mitch Webster hit a two-out homer in the ninth to tie it. Our dugout gave Mitch probably the happiest greeting he's ever had in baseball. And even though we lost the game, 6-5, in the bottom of the 10th, there was something about Mitch's home run that helped us shrug off the final score and look forward to the next day.

June 4

It really was as if Mitch's homer the day before inspired us. In the third game against the Cards, we hit six home runs, two by Shawon, two by Ryno, and one each by Mitch and Vance Law. That set a record for Busch Stadium. There was some bad blood, going back to last season, between Mark Grace and Frank DiPino. So when DiPino came in to relieve Scott Terry, who had given up two straight homers, the first hitter he faced was Mark and he threw his first pitch high and tight. Mark charged the mound and both benches joined the brawl. I started out, but John Fiero told me to sit down; if you're on the disabled list, you aren't allowed on the field during the game. It wasn't much of a fight, but Mark ended up partially separating his right shoulder and that was bad news for us. Mark said later that he'd heard that DiPino had been talking about throwing at him. So we got the win, 11-3, but lost our star first baseman for the next 18 days in the process.

June 5

We started a seven-game homestand in just the right way—by beating the Mets, 15-3. Dwight hit his first major league homer—with two on—along with a double, a single, and a walk, and Mitch Webster homered for the third straight day—pretty soon people would be calling him "Babe." David Cone started for the Mets and he's a good pitcher—he's got a sinker, a slider, a good fastball, and he spots the ball well. Beating him and clubbing the Mets was extra fun because we knew that they were one of the teams we had to beat and it was great to whip 'em good.

Sut signed an extension to his contract and he told the press: "This is a good ball club and it's only going to get better."

June 6

I said goodbye to my teammates and left for injury rehabilitation in Des Moines. Now I would be able to test my leg and work on getting my timing back at the plate and in the outfield. It was great to be able to play again and I got to see my friends on the Iowa team and to see what Triple-A is all about. I played in four games and had six hits, including a double and a homer, in 18 at-bats. I stole a couple of bases and everything felt fine.

Meanwhile, back at Wrigley, the Cubs beat the Mets again, 8-4. Dwight and Lloyd had home runs for us and in the fifth we scored three on five straight singles before Vance Law hit into a triple play. I could just hear the guys kidding about that after the game.

June 7

The wind was blowing out and even though we

scored four against Doc Gooden in the second, the Mets stormed back to win, 10-5. Lloyd's three hits, including his fourth home run, lifted his batting average to .395. He was playing first now and was doing a good job defensively as well.

June 8

It was another exciting game against the Mets. We were ahead, 3-1, at the end of four as McClendon homered for the third day in a row and we led, 4-3, in the ninth when Kevin McReynolds hit one out off of Mitch to tie the game. In the 10th, Lloyd reached on an error, Curtis Wilkerson singled, and Shawon was hit by a pitch to load the bases. Rick Wrona's squeeze bunt scored the winning run. How many catchers do you think can squeeze bunt? And how many managers can you name who would have their catcher squeeze bunt? This team was definitely having fun.

The Mets left town and in came the Cardinals— and their fans.

June 9-10-11

Jose DeLeon and Scott Sanderson threw four-hitters but two of the Cardinals' were back-to-back doubles, producing a run in the first inning and that was the game: St. Louis 1, Chicago 0. DeLeon struck out 10 Cubs. He pretty much had our number.

The next day, it was Joe Magrane throwing the shutout at us as we lost again, 6-0. McClendon had two of our six hits, but we couldn't solve Magrane that day. I got back to Chicago from Iowa and I couldn't wait to get back to my place in center field.

Doug Dascenzo and Phil Stephenson were optioned to Iowa so that I could be put on the active roster on the 11th and Andre on the 12th. It was great to play again; unfortunately, the Cardinals had a seven-run seventh inning and beat us, 10-7. Ryno, Vance, and Lloyd had homers, but it wasn't enough. The fans in the bleachers gave me a nice welcome back and so did my teammates. I was starting to think of center field at Wrigley as my home.

June 12

Steve Wilson got his first major league start because Rick's back was bothering him again. Wilson is a fierce competitor and, when he's on the mound, he is all concentration. He pitched the first five innings, left with a 6-3 lead, and we went on to win, 10-3.

I was seeing the ball real well and my swing was fluid, so I was able to get four hits to go with Ryno's three-run homer and double. Winning the last game of the series and avoiding the sweep made the plane ride to New York a lot more enjoyable than it might have been. So did the fact that Andre came off the D.L. that day. That meant that we had survived injuries to our starting outfield and now found ourselves not only still in the race, but in first place.

June 13

Andre was back in the lineup on this night. As he put it, "It feels good to feel good." And although he was 0-for-3, his sacrifice fly in the sixth allowed me to score from third with what proved to be the winning run as we beat Ron Darling and the Mets, 4-2, at Shea. Mike Bielecki pitched six-and-one-third innings of great ball and then Mitch came in and held them hitless the rest of the way.

June 14

As if it wasn't bad enough that Doc Gooden was pitching, it rained hard enough to shorten the game to six-and-a-half innings and allowed the Mets to escape with a 2-0 win. Sanderson went all the way for us and he summed up our feelings about the game to reporters in the clubhouse: "I don't like losses."

June 15

This might have been the most miserable night of the season. Counting rain delays, the game took 12 innings and five-and-a-half hours on getaway night— all in a losing cause. We were ahead, 3-0, in the eighth and ahead, 3-1, in the ninth with two out and two strikes on Dave Magadan, when he tied the game with a bases-loaded single off of Mitch. Then in the 12th, Gregg Jefferies singled with two on and two out to give the Mets the win, 4-3. By the time we were on the plane for Montreal, the frustration had died down and we were looking ahead and forgetting what had just happened. Instead of winning three out of four from the Mets, we had to settle for a split. It also gave the Mets a kind of lift and that's the last thing we wanted to do.

June 16

This was the night we fell out of first place by a half game for the first time since May 23. We got behind early and after trailing, 7-2, in the sixth, we ended up losing, 8-5. Dwight had three hits and Ryno had two, including his 10th homer. It wasn't enough, though. Zim shrugged it off by saying, "All it means is that for now everybody's chasing the Expos." Hubie Brooks told reporters that even if a lot of people didn't think the Cubs were for real, he did. He was right!

June 17

I didn't know if Zim was going to say "now they're chasing the Cubs again," but we moved back into first place the next night with a 3-2 win over Pascual

Perez. We were behind, 2-0, in the fifth and then Andre, Damon, and Vance all doubled and the game was tied. In the seventh, I got a hit to bring Domingo Ramos home with what proved to be the winning run. When you're having a good year, things like that happen for you. You have to go up there relaxed when you're at bat with men on base. You can't go up saying, "I gotta do this" or "I gotta do that." You have to be loose to hit.

And you have to be great to do what Ryno did in the ninth. The bases were loaded and Spike Owen hit a smash on the ground toward right. Ryno reacted as quickly as the ball was hit, knocked it down, picked it up, and threw Owen out. You need those kind of plays if you're going to win in the big leagues.

June 18

Andre Dawson, who had been struggling a little since returning to the lineup, blasted a three-run homer to the deepest part of center field in the first inning and we were on our way to another exciting win, 5-4. I had a good day running and I stole four bases, one short of the Cub record, but it really wasn't that great of a feat because Mark Langston has that big kick before he delivers to the plate and that's an invitation to run. We felt good about taking two of three from Montreal. Next...on to Pittsburgh.

June 20

This was one of those strange back-and-forth games that are fun to play in—if you win them. We were leading, 3-2, in the eighth when Van Slyke hit a long drive that was between me and Andre. You don't call for those kind of balls, you both just go for it and hope that one of you will reach it. In Pittsburgh that wall isn't so high that you can't go up and steal a homer. I jumped in front of the wall and I came down with it in my glove, but Andre's momentum forced him to bump me as he was going past and I dropped the ball. Van Slyke made it to third and then scored when R.J. Reynolds singled after Bonilla had walked. Then the Pirates went ahead when Gary Redus got a hit to right field. We came back in the ninth when Dwight pinch-hit a triple and Damon drove him home to tie it up. It stayed that way until the 11th when Shawon, who had been on the bench because of a sore hamstring, drove in Vance with the winning run. Andre hit his seventh homer and I hit my third to help the cause as we won, 5-4.

June 21

We did it again in 11 innings the next night, this time, 1-0, behind Greg Maddux and Mitch. Gary Varsho led off the 11th with a double off of Doug Bair, went to third on Damon's sacrifice fly, and scored on Lloyd's fly to right. Who says you can't win with pitching, defense, and speed? And who says that isn't exciting baseball?

June 22

We picked up our sixth win in the nine-game road trip by sweeping the Pirates, 8-0, behind Rick Sutcliffe. Again Damon, Dwight, and Ryno led the way. I felt that I was making a contribution; I had gone 18-for-46 (.391) in 11 games since returning to the lineup and raised my season's average to .284. And I had eight stolen bases in that time and that was a good sign that my speed was back and my leg was sound. We came home in first place with a three-game lead over the Mets. As soon as we got home, Mark Grace would be back on the active list. Everything was looking smooth.

June 23-24-25

It didn't work out the way we had planned. Montreal came in and swept three from us. In the first one, ex-Cub Dave Martinez hit two home runs and Langston, big kick and all, held us to four hits. The final score was 5-1. But there was good news that day, too. Mark Grace was activated and so we had one of our key players back. Mark adds to our hitting attack, but he also plays with confidence and you know you can count on him in pressure situations.

The next day Kevin Gross shut us out on three hits, 5-0. Gross is a tough pitcher when he is on target and this must have been one of his best games of the year. Paul Kilgus gave up five runs in the fifth inning and that was the game. Les Lancaster, called up that day to replace Pat Perry who had been put on the disabled list, pitched three good innings in relief and that was the highlight of the day for us.

In game three, it was Dennis Martinez who shut us out on five hits, 5-0. Poor Scott Sanderson pitched well enough to win, but we were having a team slump at the plate. Even though it was a low scoring game, it took more than three hours to complete. Scott and Rick both pitch very deliberately.

———————

It's hard to play behind someone who takes a lot of time between pitches. It makes it just that much harder to keep your concentration in the field. You have to move around because if you stand in one place, the temptation is to relax and the next thing you know, you're back on your heels and not ready to make the play if the ball is hit to you.

As the season went on, I learned more where to play the hitters in the league. Even though our outfield coach Joe Martinez moved me in, back, or over, and Andre would call me over to tell me to adjust here or there, as centerfielder I am the captain of the outfield. I don't often pull rank on Andre; he's got eight more Gold Glove awards than I do, but he expects me to make the calls out there and I'm not afraid to do so.

We were glad to see the Expos leave and we thought we were ready to host the Pirates.

June 26

If Doug Drabek had pitched against everybody like he did this year against the Cubs, he'd win the Cy Young Award. We hit him pretty well this time— seven hits in all—but our only run came in the fifth when I doubled Vance home with two out. Meanwhile, Bonds had opened the game with a triple for the Pirates and scored on Belliard's single. A double and a groundout got Belliard home for a 2-0 lead. We didn't think much of it at the time and Greg Maddux didn't allow another run or hit for the rest of the game. The 2-1 loss dropped us back to second place. Zim told the press: "I'm not going to cut my throat because we've lost four games. We have to wade through it now, that's all."

Zim was a patient manager all year. With all of the injuries and hot streaks and slumps and personnel changes, he was working overtime to get the best out of our talent. He didn't get down on us—he didn't jump all over us if we made a mistake—and that really helped keep the team loose. If you made a bad mistake, he'd talk to you privately, but not in anger.

And we also knew that he was deflecting the

media away from us. He didn't buy the attitude that we were playing over our heads or that we were going to drop out of the race before long. He wasn't going to panic and neither were we. His solution was simple: "We have to start hitting and start scoring, that's all."

June 27

We hit a little better and scored a little more the next day but it still wasn't quite enough. We lost, 5-4, and slipped to one-and-a-half games behind. We came back with two in the eighth on hits by Shawon and Damon, but the rally fell short and Landrum gained the save for Pittsburgh. This was definitely not fun. Still, the mood in the clubhouse wasn't tense or deflated. We knew we'd snap out of it and get back on track.

June 28

We began to wonder if the luck would ever turn. The Pirates beat us again, 3-1. No one scored through six. We took the lead in the seventh when Mark scored on a passed ball. We figured maybe, just maybe, our luck had turned. But then the Pirates scored two in the eighth off of Mike Bielecki and another in the ninth off of Mitch and we weren't able to answer. We had lost all six games on the home-stand and dropped to two-and-a-half games out, in second place. In those six games, we scored a grand total of seven runs while giving up 25. Maybe even our fans were happy to see us hit the road.

We knew we had a lot of baseball left. We never were afraid that we were going to fall on our faces. We knew that we had been playing better baseball on the road than we had at home at that point of the season, so we figured we'd be okay as soon as we got out of town.

June 29

This was the first time I had played at Candlestick and I can't say that it was very much fun. We fell behind, 7-0, in the second inning. Kilgus and Pico gave up a total of eight hits in that inning. They got five more in the eighth while all we could manage was a total of two. Zim had rested Andre, Ryno, Shawon, Vance, and Damon, probably hoping that the bench could get our offense going. The one bright spot was that Joe Girardi hit his first major league home run. The 12-2 loss dropped us to third, two-and-a-half games out.

June 30

We ended the month on an up note and broke our seven-game losing streak at the same time by beating the Giants, 6-4. I was 0-for-4 which didn't make me happy, but Ryno and Vance had two hits each and Scott, Steve Wilson, and Mitch did the job on the mound. It was Ryno's 1,000th game, qualifying him as the all-time leading infielder at second base with a .988 lifetime percentage. It's a pleasure to watch him every day.

Despite the fact that we had been through a tough stretch, we still enjoyed a pretty good June. Those who thought that we were on our way down just didn't know this team.

National League East Standings
June 30, 1989

	W	L	Pct.	GB
Montreal	44	35	.557	—
New York	40	35	.533	2
CHICAGO	41	37	.526	$2^{1/2}$
St. Louis	38	37	.507	4
Pittsburgh	33	41	.446	$8^{1/2}$
Philadelphia	27	48	.360	15

Still Flyin' High in July

7

July 1

Greg Maddux is a tough player and, for a pitcher, a pretty good hitter. I guess he decided to get us off to a good start in July because he had two hits in three trips, scored a run, and drove in another while he pitched into the eighth, allowing two runs on seven hits and leading us to a 3-2 win. It was Reuschel on the mound for the Giants, so it was extra special when Greg's single drove Vance in with what was to be the winning run in the fourth inning. The Giants have a great team and it gave us an extra boost to beat them, especially in their own park. I went 2-for-5 with a double and a stolen base. Dwight and Mark had two hits, too, so we were getting back on track.

July 2

We had them beat again at Candlestick. We were ahead, 3-0, in the bottom of the sixth, thanks to a third-inning double by Rick—who then scored on my single—and an inning later to a run-scoring double by Shawon. We were still ahead in the bottom of the eighth when Will Clark singled Butler home to cut our lead to 3-2. There were two outs and we were hanging on for dear life. Then Kevin Mitchell hit a long home run to right field and Bedrosian came in to close us out in the ninth and give the Giants a 4-3 win. That one really hurt. Jim Frey told the press, "When you lose a game like that, it's easy to go on a losing streak."

This was a short road trip and we split four games with the Giants. Now we were going back to Wrigley for six games before the All-Star break. Mitchell's homer was a distant memory by the time we landed at O'Hare. But what we remembered of it we didn't like.

July 4

We proved right away that this homestand would be different from the last one. We moved back into a tie with the Mets, two games behind Montreal, by beating the Padres, 5-1. Zim moved Ryno into the second spot in the lineup for the first time this season. Even though I didn't get on my first time up, Ryno singled, Dwight walked, and Andre singled, sending Dwight to third. Then Damon singled home Andre and we had all we needed. Mike Bielecki and Steve Wilson held the Padres in check and we won, 5-1. Even if we had to work on the Fourth of July— we liked it.

What was most important about this game was that once again we came back from a tough loss and played the game like it was Opening Day. A different team, a lesser team, might have gone into a psychological slump when Mitchell beat us in San Fran-

cisco. But we came right back and beat a good pitcher
in Ed Whitson.

July 5

On Wednesday the Padres got off to a big start
against us, scoring three runs in the first. But that's
our thing; we like scoring early. So we got two back
right away in the bottom of the first when I scored
ahead of Mark on his third homer of the season. In
the third Mark drove me home again with what
proved to be the winning run in our 5-3 victory. Mark
had three doubles and a homer in four trips and I had
three hits in four trips, including a bunt hit and a
double, and scored twice—which is what I am supposed to do. Scott Sanderson pitched well for five
innings and then Paul Kilgus shut them out the rest
of the way.

It was announced that same day that Ryno was
voted as the starting second baseman for the 1989
N.L. All-Star team. Ryno is a quiet guy. I get along
with him great and I can joke with him. I have
enormous respect for the way he plays the game.
There are a lot of balls that I think are coming
through to right center that never make it that far
because he glides over and cuts them off and throws
the runners out. I studied him at the plate all season.
He has the ideal compact swing; he comes through
the zone quickly and with power. I've studied Ryno
from different angles when he's at the plate—from
the dugout and from being on first or second base—
and I think his swing is one of the best in the game.
He's a player and, even though he's quiet, he's a
leader. I like to think that once he was moved up to
second in the batting order, he saw some better
pitches to hit because I was on base and they didn't

want me to steal. That's how a team uses each person's strength to help the other and thereby help the team as a whole.

July 6

I went 0-for-5 in the third game with the Padres, but fortunately it didn't matter. Ryno, Andre, and Shawon each homered and we got off to a 4-1 lead in the third and finished with a 7-3 win. Once again, Maddux pitched well and Mitch came on to finish with a save. Andre and Mitch were both named to the All-Star team and we were all happy for them.

July 7

We had the Dodgers back for three games and started off the series by scoring three in the second and going on to post a 6-4 win. I saw the ball extremely well in this game and went 2-for-4 with three RBIs. It's a bonus when I can drive in runs because as a leadoff hitter that isn't part of my job description.

Having a good day and winning is my idea of a good time. There were lots of things about this game that made it interesting. Rick went six innings and got his 10th win; Les Lancaster struck out the first two men in the seventh and then Zim took him out and brought in Steve Wilson to face Kirk Gibson. The fans booed Zim at the time, but Steve got Gibson on a fly to left. After the game, Zim joked about the fans, saying that they all think they're managers and that's what makes it fun. Mitch came in to pitch the last five outs, including a strikeout of Gibson to end the game. He had pitched to Kirk when they were both in the American League and Mitch claimed that Gibson never hit him—like everybody else back then, Kirk didn't dig in on him because, as Mitch put it, "back then I was wild."

July 8

We had 12 hits, but scored only twice while the Dodgers were racking up eight runs and altogether it was a bad game. Lloyd pinch-hit a homer, but other than that there wasn't much to cheer for: L.A. 8, Chicago 2.

After the game, Dwight and I talked to Andre for a while. He is like a brother to us. We can talk to him anytime and he always lets us know that the more relaxed we are the better we'll play.

Mental preparation is a big part of the game of baseball. After an at-bat you have a good sense of what you did right or wrong and what you need to do to hit better the next time up. I took the tape of my at-bats during that day's game and studied it. I had some wood on the ball, but nevertheless went 0-for-5. I knew that I'd do better tomorrow.

July 9

We beat Valenzuela the next day and had fun doing it. When you're at home and the crowd gets into it, it really gets you going and you can put together some innings. We had a big crowd that Sunday and didn't waste any time giving the fans something to cheer about. We put six runs up in the first three innings and went on to an 11-4 rout. Damon led the way with 2-for-5, a homer, and four RBIs. Andre was 3-for-5 with two RBIs and I had 2-for-5 and scored twice and batted one in. This was the last game before the All-Star break and we really wanted to win it. Here we were, a little better than half way through the season, and we were in second place with a 47-39 record and trailing the Expos by only one-and-a-half games.

If you're not playing in the All-Star game, you get three days off and it's a great time to kick back and relax a bit. I watched the game on TV and I wish our guys had pulled it out. But it was fun to realize that Ryno, Andre, Rick, and Mitch weren't just stars, they were my teammates. I'd be more than happy one of these years to give up the three-day vacation for a chance to play in the All-Star game.

July 13

Have you ever had one of those days when everything seemed to be going right and wrong at the same time? That's what happened to me this Thursday night in San Diego. I had four hits in four trips to the plate, but I was picked off of first, thrown out stealing home, caught at third trying to stretch a double into a triple, and, to top it off, I sprained my ankle. There were, however, a couple of things that eased the pain considerably: one, we won, 7-3, for Greg Maddux and secondly, despite my adventures, I scored one run and drove in two to help. Talk about mixed bag...The paper said that I just missed running for the cycle!

July 14

Before Friday's game, Zim talked to me in his office about my baserunning mistakes. The press reported that I had "provoked his ire." But that's not the way it was. Zim had been in my corner all the way and he just told me to use my head and take it a base at a time and that I have to do a better job on the bases. I wasn't sure why, but the only mistakes I seemed to be forcing then were my own.

My ankle was still really sore that night, so I couldn't play. The Padres got seven runs in the first six innings and put us away, 7-3. Mike Bielecki, who usually owns San Diego, didn't have it that evening. Still, that was only the second time in 10 games this season that the Padres had beaten us.

I wanted to earn Zim's confidence and get the green light to steal more. I hadn't shown it the day before, but I know the fundamentals of baserunning real well. You couldn't play for Coach Powell for two years and not know what to do on the bases. He worked on it until he knew we had it and then he worked on it some more. I remember times in the spring when it would be freezing cold—and I hate cold weather— and he'd take the team to first base with his clipboard in hand and he'd talk about baserunning at first—how to lead off the base, how to cut the corner if you were going on to second, and so on. These were the pointers that he'd learned over the years and he meant us to have them. Then we'd move to second base and Coach would spend a half hour there talking about the main points and the fine points of baserunning with second as the focus. Then we'd go to third and he'd teach us about third and, then to home plate.

When I got to the majors there really wasn't anything I hadn't heard before because Coach Powell has taught us so thoroughly.

In my first year of college ball, I remember we had lost a couple of games due to poor sliding. We got back from a game about 8:00 P.M. or so and Coach said we needed some practice. He had us in the outfield, sliding head first back and forth, and about half the team decided to quit. He looked at me a few days later and said, "Jerome, if you want to quit, you can leave, too." I said, "No, Coach, I don't want to quit. But I do want to go see my little boy." (Jonathan was there to visit me.) And he said, "Okay, well, we'll be through in a few minutes." I'm glad Coach Powell taught us as well as he did. I was never even tempted to quit.

In the major leagues you need to learn how to read the pitchers. I watch Ryno a lot. He's fast, but he's not that fast. He knows how to get great jumps off of first. He steals even when they know he's going to. The other thing that was new up in the majors was that you are up against better arms than you've ever challenged before and you can tell that the fielders take it real seriously. The day before, I was trying to be too aggressive and I ran into some mistakes. I figured I'd probably run into some more before the year was over, but I'd get better too.

***

July 15

Ryno and Dwight hit home runs in the first inning and it looked like we were off and running. And then we didn't score again. I went 0-for-4 against Walt Terrell, who should not have been exactly mystifying. Meanwhile, the Padres scored two in the second and one in the eighth and hung on to win, 3-2. We were still in a tie for second with the Mets, two-and-a-half games behind Montreal, but this was not the kind of game you ought to lose.

July 16

Another close one and our third straight loss to the Padres. We scored three in the sixth when Mitch Webster singled in front of Lloyd's ninth homer. Then Mark doubled and Rick Sutcliffe singled. But the Padres got two in the second and two more in the sixth and, almost before we knew it, the game was gone, 4-3. This was our last game of the season with San Diego and we finished with an 8-4 advantage, but we should not have lost the last three. We dropped to three-and-a-half games out.

Zim wasn't upset. He didn't even mind it when we joked around on the bus going to the airport to board the plane for Los Angeles. He told the press later, "I hear guys kidding each other on the bus and, as long as we go about it in the right way, they can still have fun and laugh on the bus, even if we lose three in a row. But when you're going good and winning some games, I don't care what team you watch, there is that little edge of having even more fun."

July 17

We had more fun the next night, as a matter of fact. I led off the game with a hit; Ryno moved me up to second and Mark drove us both home with a long home run into center field. Almost always when we got a good lead in the first or second inning, we'd go on to win the game. That held up that Monday night in L.A., even though the Dodgers tied us at three in the sixth. In the eighth we got three more when Curtis Wilkerson worked a walk with the bases full, Andre hit a sacrifice fly, and Domingo poked a run-scoring single to left. We won, 6-3. It was Les Lancaster's first victory. He had pitched incredibly well for us since coming back from Iowa. Everybody had a lot of confidence in him.

July 18

Orel Hershiser finally beat us once after two losses to us earlier in the season. I didn't hit him in four trips and we only got four hits off of him altogether. Meanwhile, the Dodgers got four runs off of Greg in six innings and put the game away, 4-1.

This wasn't the kind of loss that, like a bad hamburger, stayed with us for a long time. We lost to a great pitcher that day and the law of averages says that someone with his stuff is going to beat you at least one out of three if you're lucky.

July 19

We ended our road trip at 3-4 with a 4-0 victory over the Dodgers on a brilliant three-hitter by Mike Bielecki. He had great mastery of his stuff and they couldn't get a beat on him. Meanwhile, Vance Law went 3-for-4 with a double and a triple and Mitch Webster had three hits—including a double—in five trips. The whole team was happy for both Vance and Mitch. These guys were both starters the year before and Vance had had the best year of his career. Now, this year, they were part-time players. But neither of them was bitter. They didn't hang their heads or make excuses. They are both great team players. Dwight told me that Mitch said to him, "You deserve to be starting. Keep it up, you're doing a great job." If you want to get a definition of what a real team is, study the 1989 Cubs.

We were ready to go home.

July 20

This might have been one of the most important games of the season. The Giants had scored three runs off of Paul Kilgus in six innings and, despite the

Cubs 4, Giants 3

	ab	r	h	bi		ab	r	h	bi
Butler cf	5	1	2	0	Walton cf	5	0	0	0
R. Thmpsn 2b	5	0	2	1	Sandberg 2b	5	0	1	0
W. Clark 1b	5	0	0	0	Webster rf	4	0	1	0
Maldonado rf	5	2	2	0	Grace 1b	4	1	1	0
Litton 3b	3	0	0	0	Berryhill c	5	1	1	0
Bedrosn p	0	0	0	0	McClendon lf	4	0	2	0
Riles ph	1	0	0	0	Law 3b	2	0	0	0
Gossage p	0	0	0	0	D. Smith lf	3	1	1	1
McCmnt p	0	0	0	0	Dunston ss	2	0	0	0
D.Nixon lf	4	0	1	1	Wilkerson ss	3	1	2	2
Sheridan lf	0	0	0	0	Kilgus p	1	0	0	0
Manwaring c	3	0	1	0	Varsho ph	1	0	0	0
Uribe ss	5	0	2	0	Pico p	0	0	0	0
LaCoss p	3	0	0	0	Dawson ph	1	0	1	0
Oberkfl 3b	2	0	0	0	Schiraldi p	0	0	0	0
					Ramos ph	1	0	0	0
					Lancaster p	1	0	1	1
Totals	**41**	**3**	**10**	**2**	**Totals**	**42**	**4**	**11**	**4**

```
San Francisco          010  110  000  00—3
CUBS                   000  000  003  01—4
```

E—Law, McClendon, Maldonado, Berryhill. DP—San Francisco 1. LOB—San Francisco 9, CUBS 9. 2B—Webster, Maldonado 2, Uribe, Lancaster. 3B—Butler. S—Litton, Manwaring.

	IP	H	R	ER	BB	SO
San Francisco						
LaCoss	7	3	0	0	1	9
Bedrosn	2	5	3	2	0	2
Gossage	2/3	0	0	0	2	1
McCament L, 1-1	1	3	1	1	0	0
CUBS						
Kilgus	6	7	3	2	0	6
Pico	2	1	0	0	0	2
Schiraldi	1	0	0	0	1	1
Lancaster W, 2-0	2	2	0	0	0	1

WP—Kilgus.

Umpires—Home, Montague; First, Hohn; Second, Marsh; Third, West.

T—3:32 A—32,306.

fact that Jeff Pico had shut them down through the eighth, we were losing, 3-0, in the bottom of ninth. Up to this point in the season, we hadn't been good at coming from behind in the late innings. In fact, we were the only major league team that hadn't had a late comeback victory: we were 0-32 when losing after the sixth. And Steve Bedrosian was looking to save the shutout and the win for Mike LaCoss.

With Mark on second and Damon on first and two outs in the ninth, Dwight Smith came up. He'd been cheering the guys on from the dugout and saying, "Hey, let's get that to 1-and-31!" Now he had his chance and he drove a single to right, scoring Mark and moving Damon to third. When Maldonado threw home trying to get Mark, Dwight roared into second. Next up was Curtis Wilkerson. The crowd—now down to about 20,000 (from 32,000) who had stayed until the ninth—really got going. It was like this was the rally they'd been waiting for all season. Curtis is a tough little guy; he stands in there and takes his cuts. When he drove an 0-and-2 fastball for a single into center field, Damon and Dwight came around to score and the game was tied. Zim brought in Les to pitch the 10th. He had yet to give up a run since being called up on June 24. Neither team scored in the 10th and the Giants failed in their half of the 11th. Lloyd singled, leading off the bottom of the inning. Zim decided to have Dwight hit away and some of the fans were yelling at him from the box seats. They got louder when Dwight grounded into a double play. That brought up Curtis and he hit the first pitch for a single. That brought up Les, who is not exactly a feared hitter. The Giants were playing him to swing late and instead he was right on time. The ball went down the left-field line and Curtis came all the way around to score the winning run. The fans weren't the only ones going nuts. I was on deck when Les got the hit and it was just as well he did—I was 0-for-5, even though I had hit the ball hard. It hadn't been my lucky day. Until we won, 4-3.

As I look back on that game, I can see a definite upswing in our confidence that we could come back late in any game and win it. From that point on, we won 11 more in our last at-bat.

For Curtis, it was a chance to contribute and to show everybody—Zim, his teammates, and the fans—what he could do. Utility players have their pride too. I saw some pretty awesome displays of team spirit this year. Take Mitch Webster, for example. Like I mentioned, he was a starter when the season opened and then he lost his job to Dwight and Lloyd. He never hung his head. He rooted for the guys who were in there and kept himself ready—physically and mentally—for when he might be needed. Curtis, Domingo, Doug, Gary Varsho, Rick, Joe, Vance, all of the guys who might not have been able to play as much as they wanted to, all gave their best to the team effort. That, as much as anything, was why we did as well as we did.

July 21
You had to hand it to the Giants. They watched us celebrate after rallying to beat them the night before but they came right back the next day, scored all of their runs in the third inning, and hung on for a 4-3 win. We got one back in the third when I doubled Shawon home and then in the eighth Mark Grace hit one out with Dwight on base and it looked like we might pull it out again. But Lefferts came in and shut us down. Before the game, Dwight sang the National Anthem and he was great. It turned out that my

double that day was the start of my hitting streak. I hope Dwight sings more often next year.

July 22

We got off to a good start on Saturday against Atlee Hammaker, who is a finesse pitcher. If he's going to beat you, he has to keep the screwball on the outside. Vance hit two homers and Andre had one with Mark on base. We were up, 3-1, in the second. I drove in our final run with my only hit in four trips. Scott pitched really well and Les closed out the last two innings as we won, 5-2, in game three of the home series with the Giants.

July 23

Andre hit a three-run homer on Sunday and Mark had two hits and three RBIs as we clubbed the Giants, 9-5. We beat Don Robinson, who throws pretty hard and has a good slider. Greg gave up seven hits in five and a third but only three runs. He wasn't as sharp as he usually is, so Zim went to Steve Wilson and Calvin to finish the game. Calvin had one of those outings where he gave up two runs but also struck out four hitters in two innings. It felt really good to take three out of four from the leaders of the Western Division. I was hitting the ball well, but I wanted to start having some multiple hit days.

We were off to St. Louis and a lot of our fans came with us. It's like a travelling circus when Chicago invades St. Louis or they come to our place. The hotel lobby is always full of people wearing Cub hats and jackets and calling encouragement to us.

July 24

Shawon had been really hitting lately and on Monday he went 3-for-3 and scored two of our three runs. I drove him in once, with a single in the third.

Mike Bielecki really helped us out with two great sacrifice bunts and some clutch pitching. He surprised a lot of people. His 10-5 record was one of the best in the league. But he's a guy who's worked hard to get here; he's done his time in the minors and winter ball and he's a fighter. We were tied for second with the Mets, three and a half behind Montreal.

July 25

We won again in front of a full house at Busch Stadium. We scored two in the second and one in the fifth and ninth for a 4-2 victory. Paul Kilgus seems to pitch his best ball against the Cardinals. Mitch got his 25th save but not without giving us a scare by allowing a run in the ninth.

Shawon continued his hot hitting with a home run. I kept my streak going, but I think I try too hard to hit it on the ground and take advantage of the carpet and it turns out that I hit soft liners to the infielders instead.

July 26

Our winning streak got stopped at four. Jose DeLeon, with help from Ken Daley and Todd Worrell, held us to two hits. Somebody ought to talk to Jim Frey about getting DeLeon on our side. I don't know if it's psychological when a pitcher has a lot of success against a particular team, but I know that if that pitcher doesn't have good stuff on any particular day, psychology alone won't keep that team from hitting him. Rick pitched a good game for us, but we lost, 2-0. Still, if you can win two of three from your strongest competitors, you're going to be okay.

July 28

What a game! It was Shawon's day on Friday. The Mets and 37,000 Cub fans were at Wrigley Field to see what real baseball is. The Mets had a 5-2 lead in

the seventh with David Cone on the mound. Then Vance singled, Shawon singled, and I got Vance home with a sacrifice fly. Ryno singled Shawon home and then Dwight hit a homer into the right-field bleachers and we had them, 6-5. They made some noise in the ninth when Samuel singled with one out and Howard Johnson was up against Mitch. Johnson hit a blooper into short left field. Shawon raced out

Cubs 6, Mets 5

	ab	r	h	bi		ab	r	h	bi
M. Wilson cf	5	0	1	0	Walton cf	3	0	1	1
Magadn 1b	3	1	1	0	Sandberg 2b	4	2	2	1
Samuel ph	1	0	1	0	D. Smith lf	4	1	1	2
H. Johnson 3b	4	1	1	3	Grace 1b	3	0	1	0
Strawberry rf	4	1	1	0	Dawson rf	4	0	0	0
McReynolds lf	4	1	2	0	Berryhill c	4	1	2	0
Jefferies 2b	4	0	1	0	Law 3b	3	1	1	0
Carter c	3	0	0	0	Dunston ss	4	1	3	1
Elster ss	4	0	2	2	Sanderson p	1	0	0	0
Cone p	3	1	1	0	Pico p	0	0	0	0
Aguilera p	0	0	0	0	McClnd ph	1	0	0	0
Hernandez ph	1	0	0	0	Schiraldi p	0	0	0	0
Innis p	0	0	0	0	Webster ph	1	0	0	0
					Lancaster p	0	0	0	0
					M. Williams p	0	0	0	0
Totals	36	5	11	5	**Totals**	32	6	11	5

New York   005 000 000—5
CUBS   110 000 40x—6

E—H. Johnson. DP—New York 1, CUBS 1. LOB—New York 7, CUBS 5. 2B—Sandberg, Berryhill, Magadan, Elster. HR—H. Johnson (26), Dw. Smith (4). SB—Walton (14), Dunston (15). S—Law. SF—Walton.

	IP	H	R	ER	BB	SO
New York						
Cone	6²/³	8	4	4	0	4
Aguilera L,6-5	¹/³	2	2	2	1	0
Innis	1	1	0	0	0	0
CUBS						
Sanderson	2¹/³	8	5	5	0	0
Pico	1²/³	1	0	0	1	0
Schiraldi W, 3-4	3	0	0	0	2	2
Lancaster	²/³	1	0	0	0	0
M. Williams S, 26	1¹/³	1	0	0	0	0

Umpires—Home, Williams; First, McSherry; Second, West; Third, Crawford.
T—2:52 A—37,554.

full speed and caught it with his back to the infield. Then he wheeled and threw to first, doubling off Samuel to end the game. That's the kind of play that winners make—especially when the game is on the line. So was Dwight's homer.

July 29

Gary Varsho was sent down to Iowa the previous day and Darrin Jackson was called up. They are both good ballplayers and real competitors; they'd be playing regularly on some teams in the majors.

Wrigley Field probably can't hold more than what we had on hand this Saturday—more than 38,000. And we gave the crowd something to cheer about; we beat the Mets, 10-3. Dwight went 4-for-5, Ryno 3-for-4, and I had 3-for-5 to account for 10 of our 18 hits. The Mets were the team everybody said would walk away with it. I like beating them more than any ball club.

July 30

This was a battle to the end. The Mets seemed to sense that they really needed this game and they came back from a 3-0 deficit to tie us at 4-4 in the bottom of the seventh. The game went to the relief pitchers, Aguilera for them and Lancaster for us. And it stayed tied until the bottom of the ninth when Randy Myers came in to pitch and Mark Grace hit him for a two-run homer to claim a 6-4 victory. For the second straight day, I had three hits; I was seeing the ball really well and staying in my zone. For the third straight day we put it to the Mets. There wasn't anybody on the Cubs who didn't know, as we boarded the plane for Philadelphia, that we were now one-and-a-half games out of first. And by now there wasn't one of us who didn't believe that we could win it all.

July 31

We played a doubleheader that day in Philly to make up for a game that was rained out earlier. That meant we were on the field for almost five-and-a-half hours. In the first game, it looked like we were unbeatable. Ryno had two homers, giving him 15 for the year; Damon had one and Dwight had a grand slam—and he did it as a pinch hitter. It was more fire power than we needed, as Rick pitched a three-hit complete game for his 11th win, 10-2.

All in all, it was great fun. But we got off to a bad start in game two when the Phillies hit Paul for five runs in the first three innings. We just couldn't catch them after that. Mark and I both hit homers, but with nobody on. We lost, 7-4. I don't want to pass by that home run without saying that it feels good to hit a ball that hard. I know better than to aim at the fences; I aim at the ball and, if I hit it just right, it will go out on occasion. Even if I were hitting 30 a year, I wouldn't do a special home run trot—given the fact that this was my fourth, I don't figure that I'll have to worry about that.

So we ended July with a 59-46 record. And Mark Grace was named Player of the Month in the National League for hitting .347 with 34 hits, 10 doubles, five homers, and 24 RBIs in 98 trips.

National League East Standings				
July 31, 1989				
	W	**L**	**Pct.**	**GB**
Montreal	61	44	.581	—
CHICAGO	59	46	.562	2
St. Louis	54	47	.535	5
New York	53	50	.515	7
Pittsburgh	45	59	.433	15 1/2
Philadelphia	42	62	.404	18 1/2

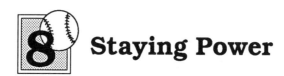

8 Staying Power

August 1

Zim called on Steve Wilson to start Tuesday night at the last minute and he really did the job. We were ahead, 4-1, when he left the game in the sixth. Les and Mitch came on to close it out by that score. Larry McWilliams was on the mound for the Phillies and, in the third inning, with Domingo and Shawon on base, he put it where I like it and I hit it to the wall in center, scoring both runners. Even though August was just beginning, we were playing every game full throttle. It was the right kind of circle—winning was fun and the fun kept us winning.

August 2

It wasn't as much fun the next night and we didn't win either. Ken Howell shut us out on three hits. His breaking ball was working perfectly. When he gets that over, he's really tough. When he doesn't, he has to come in with the fastball and you can beat him. I stayed with the curve enough that night to get one hit, but it was the Phillies' night as Dickie Thon hit two homers and Len Dykstra one. Scott gave up five runs in three-and-a-half innings and later Zim told reporters he would move Scott to the bullpen and go with a four-man rotation. Position players don't talk much about what goes on with the pitchers and nobody really wanted to second-guess Zim because we all thought his moves were working pretty good.

August 3

It was our turn to win a shutout. Greg Maddux got his 12th win, 2-0, with help from Mitch and Les. Damon's home run was all we really needed. I got a hit for a 14-game hitting streak. About the only thought I gave it was that it made me happy because I was being consistent—and that's what every hitter wants to be.

With this win, we picked up a game on the Expos and now trailed them by two. Some writer told us half-kiddingly not to peak too early. We didn't worry about that stuff.

August 4

Sometimes it looked like Zim could predict the future. Ryno and Mark each homered in the third inning to put us ahead of the Pirates and Doug Drabek, 2-0. Pittsburgh got one in the second inning and another in the third off of Mike Bielecki and it stayed tied until the ninth, when Vance Law drove in Joe Girardi. Mitch came in to pitch and Domingo came in to play third. After the first batter made an out, Cangelosi singled and then moved up to second on a wild pitch. R.J. Reynolds hit a flyball to me in center for the second out. Next up was Jeff King, who is a pretty good hitter. King drove a shot toward the hole and Domingo made a diving stop, got up, and threw to Mark who was able to tag King to end the game. Games like that are really fun when you win them. It's easier to concentrate when you know the game is on the line on any given play.

Everybody went up to Domingo and shook his hand and congratulated him. Montreal lost, so now we were a game out.

August 5

This was a game I won't forget. The ball was right there; I saw it well and my swing was everything I want it to be when I finish studying my tapes. I got three hits, but the one I was happiest about was in the third when I got a bunt hit with two out and went to second when the pitcher threw wildly. Then Ryno doubled me home to tie the game at one. The Pirates got another run in the fourth and led us, 2-1, in the top of the ninth. Their closer, Bill Landrum, had gotten us out in the eighth, but Lloyd led off the ninth with a single. Damon got a single and Vance's sacrifice fly brought in the tying run. Then Landrum threw a wild pitch, advancing the runner to second where Shawon scored him with a hit. Then Shawon surprised everyone by tagging up on Mitch Webster's long flyball and taking second after the catch. I got a hit to bring him home.

It was a good display of how we could manufacture runs using speed, surprise, and timely hitting. And when you start winning some games late, it begins to pump up your confidence and, in this game, the whole team sensed that we were about to do it again.

With one out in the ninth, Jeff King smashed a liner back at Mitch and it hit off of his left ear. Mitch went down hard and everybody was kind of stunned. John Fiero and Zim, along with some other guys, helped him up and you could see he was trying to talk

Zim into leaving him in the game. Instead, Zim brought in Les, who got the next hitter to ground into a double play and end the game.

Afterwards, Mitch was joking about it, saying that he'd been hit in the head before and that his brother used to hit him in the head all the time. Zim said that Mitch would probably be bowling that night. Everybody was feeling great. We were playing well, the breaks were going our way, and our come-from-behind win moved us into a tie for first place.

August 6

One of the things about baseball is that it doesn't take long to bring you back to earth. Paul Kilgus was supposed to start that Sunday afternoon, but he had to leave to be with his wife, who was about to have their first child. Jeff Pico took his place and got off to a tough start as the Pirates took a 3-1 lead at the end of one. We got one in the second and another in the sixth to tie the game at three. In the top of the ninth Domingo's double scored Shawon, but Calvin gave up the tying run in the bottom of the ninth and we went to extra innings. Lots of extra innings. Scott Sanderson came in and pitched nine innings; maybe he was trying to show Zim he still was a starter. But we went scoreless for nine and, in the bottom of the 18th, Jeff King hit a home run to beat us, 5-4. It was rainy all day, the game lasted almost six hours, plus another 45-minute rain delay, and then we lost it.

It was depressing to go that long and lose—especially since we really had the game won. I don't remember what inning it was, but we had Mark Grace on third and he tagged up on a fly and came home safe. But the umpire called him out. I had three hits for the second day in a row, but that didn't matter because we didn't win. Everyone was drained and it was really quiet on the plane back to Chicago.

Yet, with this team you could almost count on us to come back from a bad loss to get a win the next day. The Expos were coming to Wrigley for three games and this game wasn't going to stop us from being ready for them.

August 7

You know when you go head-to-head with your main opposition that these are the games you really want to win. We had 39,000 of our fans at Wrigley to encourage us to a 5-2 victory. They went wild when we scored three in the third, two on a homer by Mark. I scored after a triple and a single by Dwight and also when Ryno homered in the bottom of the seventh. Greg got his 13th win. For the third straight day I had three hits; the ball looked big to me then.

Things got hot in the fifth when I hit a smash back at the mound and it hit Pascual Perez on his non-pitching arm. The second baseman threw me out and I went back into the dugout. Their trainer went out to see Perez and, the next thing you knew, Perez threw the ball into our dugout. Apparently he was trying to hit me. Sut got the ball and threw it back at Perez. I guess Perez was frustrated because he knew we were going to win and move into sole possession of first place. As Greg said, "We're happy to be in first, but at this point it doesn't really mean much."

I have to say that I don't think cockiness goes with stardom. I don't think you need to be cocky to have a positive attitude toward what you do. I am surprised by how many outfielders up here showboat by sliding to make catches they could make standing up. And also by how many guys do special trots when they hit one or special victory signs when they strike somebody out. I don't really think there's any place

for that. I don't think anybody has to show anybody else up.

August 8

As if to underline the fact that I was on a hitting binge, I was the first of three Cubs to homer off of Dennis Martinez in the second game with the Expos. Even so, it was a close game and we only won it, 4-2, behind Mike, who got his 12th win against five losses. It was a good day of streaks: It was Mike's fourth straight win, Les brought his Cub record of consecutive scoreless innings to $30^{2/3}$, and I set a record for Cub rookies by hitting in my 19th straight game. Our fans really pumped us up during this game. They had been after us to take curtain calls. They wanted me to come out in the first after my homer, but as Ryno said, "You never take a bow in the first inning." As for my homer—when Martinez missed with his slider, I figured he'd come back with a fastball so he wouldn't fall behind. He did and I was ready.

Things looked a little scary in the ninth. They had hit some zingers off of Mitch in the eighth and then I had to go to the wall to get Brooks' fly to open the ninth. When Tim Raines got a hit, Zim brought in Les. Tim Wallach hit one down the right-field line and Andre had to run a mile at full speed to catch it. Zim probably went home and said, "Just another day at the office."

August 9

Tony LaRussa came to the game that Wednesday, probably scouting both teams just in case. We gave him plenty to think about. He saw Rick pitch a masterful game, giving up only one hit and no runs in seven innings. Meanwhile, we scored when Damon's single drove in Mark in the second and Ryno homered after I had singled in the third. Mitch came in and, though he gave up three hits in two innings, preserved the shutout for a 3-0 win.

We drew the largest crowds for a three-game series in Wrigley Field history. We had swept three from our nearest competitor and I think that was when we knew that we were going to win the division. Winning like that is how you get good chemistry to be even better and then the real good chemistry is what helps you keep going. The Expos knew they weren't out of it yet. Buck Rogers, their manager, said that their next three-game series at Wrigley would be bigger than this one. We hoped so.

August 10

It seemed like almost every time we lost a really tough one, we came back to win. And every time it looked like we were on our way to a long streak, we found a way to lose one we shouldn't. On this Thursday afternoon, the Phillies were at Wrigley and the wind was blowing out. It was a day when I was glad I had given up pitching in college. We were ahead, 10-3, at the end of four. Ryno homered in his fourth consecutive game; to be on the safe side he hit one in the first and another in the third. He had four hits; so did Dwight and Shawon, while Mark and I each had two. It looked like a laugher until the Phillies scored seven in the fifth, two in the sixth, and four in the seventh to take a 16-13 win.

When the wind is blowing like that, you play a lot deeper in the outfield. It affects your throws, too, because you can put something on it one time and it dies and another time, if the wind has died down momentarily, you can put too much on it. I did that in the seventh and my error allowed a run that shouldn't have scored. You don't take a loss like that really hard because it wasn't necessarily the better team that won.

August 11

The wind died down the next afternoon and so did the Phillies. Ryno became the second Cub in history to homer in five straight games. The other was Hack Wilson, who used to play center field. I got hit by Don Carman in the first, then walked, and struck out before singling in the fifth, scoring Domingo and Shawon. Then Ryno homered and, for the fourth time in the six times he'd homered in the last five games, I was on and scored in front of him. My hitting streak was up to 22 games now and I was thinking about it mainly because everybody was reminding me of it every day. The most important fact of the day was that the Cubs won, 9-2.

August 12

The crowd got everything it wanted and then some on this Saturday. The Phillies scored three runs off of Mike Bielecki in the first inning. Ken Howell started for the Phils and he is a tough pitcher. But he wasn't at his best that day. I led off with a single to keep my streak alive at 23. Curtis struck out on the hit-and-run, but I stole second and then scored on Dwight's single. Howell walked three of the next four batters, forcing in a run and bringing up Shawon. He'd been really hot lately. He had changed his batting stance and gone back to the one he used in high school and he just started hitting. In his first time up that day, he lined the first pitch for a double to left, clearing the bases. We scored again in the second and added three in the third when Shawon homered with two on. That put us up, 9-3, and we held on to win, 9-7. The Phillies loaded the bases in the ninth off of Mitch, but he pitched his way out of it to get his 30th save. This was definitely Shawon's day and that was one of the great things about this ball club—we were glad to pass the hero label to anyone who deserved it. It seemed like every day it was someone different.

August 13

On Sunday, the Phillies scored twice in the first, but we knew we could come back so we weren't worried. In the fourth, Mark tripled and Lloyd drove him in. An inning later, Domingo walked, Sut sacrificed him to second, and I doubled him in. I was able to score on Mark's single up the middle and we led, 3-2. It stayed that way until Von Hayes led off the sixth with a long drive to straight-away center. I saw that it was going to be over my head so I turned and ran as fast as I could and then jumped to try to get it. Instead, I rammed into the wall with my left shoulder and the force snapped my head back. I fell to the ground and the ball bounced away for an inside-the-park homer to tie the game. Lloyd, John Fiero, and Zim were there in a flash—well, it took Zim a little longer than that—and after a couple of minutes, I felt well enough to stay in the game. The Phillies got two runs in the eighth and we couldn't solve reliever Jeff Parrett, so we ended up with a 5-3 loss. My shoulder stiffened up after the game, but we had an off day before playing Cincinnati and I thought it would probably be okay by then.

Somehow the Cubs need to pad that wall. The warning track helps, but if you're really going after the ball, you can't take time out to count steps. The bricks don't give.

August 15

Andre had been in a slump and I think it was mainly because he was in a lot of pain with his knees.

But on Tuesday night he hit a three-run homer in the
12th to lead us over the Reds, 5-2, at Riverfront. The
fact that the game went that long gave me an extra at-
bat in the 12th. Until then I was 0-for-5. I led off the
12th with a single off of Mike Roesler and now my
streak was at 25 games. The guys were kidding me a
lot, calling me "Joe D." and stuff, and that helped
keep me loose. When Ryno's streak of homering in
five straight games ended, he said that he was glad
it was over because it was beginning to tempt him to
swing for homers. I know what he meant. The streak
is nice, but you don't want it to change your approach.

August 16
    We beat the Reds again the next night, 5-1, and
lots of good things happened. I opened with an infield
single, took second on a ground ball, stole third, and
came home on a single by Andre. The Reds scored
one in the fourth to tie and they used up two of their
hits doings so; Mike Bielecki was unbeatable that
night. We put the game away in the sixth. Andre led
off with a homer, Damon walked, Vance doubled,
Shawon walked, and then Bielecki put down a sui-
cide squeeze bunt with two strikes and it worked.
Everybody was ribbing him later because he was
batting something like .019. He said, "I can bunt, I
just can't hit." Then I got a double to drive in two runs
and that was more than we needed. We were playing
good ball then and the mood of the team reflected it.

August 17
    It was my turn to give the club a lift. It was a game
that I'll remember for a long time. We manufactured
a run in the first when I reached on a bunt hit and
went to second when Benzinger threw wildly past
first. When Ryno grounded out, I made it to third and

then came home, thanks to Dwight who grounded to the right side. The lead held up until the bottom of the eighth because Sut was pitching one of his best games of the year.

Cubs 3, Cincinnati 2

	ab	r	h	bi		ab	r	h	bi
Walton cf	5	1	2	2	Winningham rf	3	0	1	0
Sandberg 2b	4	0	1	0	Richardson ss	2	0	0	0
D. Smith lf	4	0	0	1	Madison 3b	1	0	0	0
Grace 1b	3	0	0	0	E. Davis cf	3	1	1	2
Dawson rf	3	0	0	0	Griffey lf	3	0	1	0
Berryhill c	3	0	0	0	Franco p	0	0	0	0
Law 3b	3	0	1	0	Benzinger 1b	4	0	2	0
Wilkerson pr	0	1	0	0	Quinones 3b	2	0	0	0
Ramos 3b	0	0	0	0	J. Reed c	3	0	0	0
Dunston ss	4	1	1	0	Youngblood ph	1	0	0	0
Sutcliffe p	2	0	1	0	Oester 2b	3	0	0	0
McClendon ph	0	0	0	0	Oliver ph	1	0	0	0
M. Williams p	0	0	0	0	R. Robinson p	2	0	0	0
					Dibble p	0	0	0	0
					Collins ph	1	1	1	0
					Roomes lf	0	0	0	0
Totals	**31**	**3**	**6**	**3**	**Totals**	**29**	**2**	**6**	**2**

```
CUBS             100  000  002—3
Cincinnati       000  000  020—2
```
　　E—Benzinger. DP—CUBS 1, Cincinnati 1. LOB—CUBS 7, Cincinnati 6. 2B—Law, Sandberg. HR—E. Davis 26). SB—Winningham (9), E. Davis (13). S—Richardson, Winningham, Quinones.

	IP	H	R	ER	BB	SO
CUBS						
Sutcliffe W, 13-9	8	5	2	2	3	7
M. Williams S, 31	1	1	0	0	0	2
Cincinnati						
R. Robinson	7	4	1	0	4	2
Dibble	1	0	0	0	0	3
Franco L, 3-7	1	2	2	2	2	0

　　PB—Berryhill. Umpires—Home, Crawford; First, Williams; Second, Hohn; Third, West.
T—2:46 A—29,278.

　　　　Dave Collins led off the Reds eighth with a single but only got as far as third with two out. Then Eric Davis was up. Sut had struck him out twice, but this time he hit a tremendous home run and all of a sudden the Reds were leading, 2-1, with their star closer, John Franco, on the mound. He got the first two hitters easily and one of the guys on the bench looked up at the scoreboard and said that at least nobody would gain on us. Calvin said, "Well, this one ain't over yet." Vance Law worked Franco for a walk and Curtis ran for him. Then Shawon kept it alive with a single up the middle. Lloyd waited Franco out and walked to fill the bases. As I went up to the plate I just reminded myself to concentrate on meeting the ball solidly. His first pitch was a slider and I laid off of it for ball one. His control had been off and I knew he needed to throw his fastball to get it over. He did and I hit through the left side, scoring Curtis and Shawon. Lloyd got thrown out trying to go from first to third, but we had come back with two outs in the ninth and taken the lead. In the bottom of the ninth, Benzinger led off with a hit off of Mitch and was sacrificed to second. We didn't have to worry about trying to nail him at the plate after a hit because Mitch struck out the next two batters and we had the win. Our three-game sweep of the Reds put us four-and-a-half games ahead of the second-place Mets.

Ever since I can remember I've always wanted to be the one on the spot when the game was on the line. I remember a high school football game when we were losing, 27-17, with time running out. The coach called for a reverse and I came around from my split end position, got the ball, and took it 80 yards to the six-yard line. We scored on the next play to win the game. It was the same way in basketball. I liked the challenge of being the one to take the shot that decided whether we won or lost. They didn't always go in and sometimes I made the third out in the ninth and didn't come through. But the excitement of sports is to test your limits and that's what pumps me up.

August 18

The press had been making a big thing out of my hitting streak and the guys were really on me and giving me a lot of stuff. I was supposed to be doing calisthenics before the game, but I was doing a pre-game television interview, which was going back live to Chicago from Houston. The guys were all yelling at me—"Hey, Juice, do that on your own time!" I don't think the mike picked them up, but I couldn't keep a straight face. I must have looked pretty happy to the fans back home because I was laughing through the whole interview.

The game got under way and we scored five times in the first four innings and it looked like not even the Astrodome could stop us. In the second, Andre got his 2,000th career hit. He followed it with the 281st stolen base of his career. Earlier this season he hit his 300th major league home run. Only one player has ever had 2,000 hits, 300 homers, and 300 stolen bases and that was Willie Mays. Andre will be the second.

In the third, I got a single off of Jim Clancy and tied Ron Santo's modern Cub hitting streak record of 28 games, which he set in 1966. We were still leading, 5-2, going into the bottom of the eighth. The Astros scored twice then and twice more in the bottom of the ninth to beat us, 6-5. They got the winning run on a walk with the bases full—not a good way to end a game.

August 19

For the first time since mid-July, we lost two games in a row. The Astros beat us, 8-4, in spite of two homers by Mark Grace. We just didn't have a good game and you have to say that the Astros really know how to play in their stadium. I didn't get a hit until the seventh when I dropped one into right field. That gave me the Cub record at 29 and it's nice to think that for a while my name is in the book.

August 20

We were really glad to get out of Houston. They beat us again, 8-4, the next afternoon to complete the sweep. The game was a lot closer than the score. They led, 4-2, at the end of six and we kept chipping away. Ryno homered in the seventh and then again in the ninth and it looked like this would be one of those games where we would come back and pull it out. But then in the bottom of the ninth, Les walked Rafael Ramirez and Zim brought in Mitch. His control wasn't there and he walked Craig Reynolds and hit Gerald Young to load the bases. When he struck out Bill Doran, I thought maybe we'd have another Opening Day. But then Kevin Bass hit a grandslam homer; it was his second homer of the game. He always seems to hit well against us. We got eight hits off of Mike Scott and, when you can do that, you know that you're not exactly in a team slump. I got an infield single in the first, so my streak was up to 30. As long as I had gotten that far, I wanted to catch up with Benito Santiago's rookie record of 34.

Astros 8, Cubs 4

	ab	r	h	bi		ab	r	h	bi
Walton cf	5	0	1	0	Young cf	4	2	2	1
Sandberg 2b	4	3	3	2	Doran 2b	5	0	1	0
D. Smith lf	5	0	1	0	Bass lf	5	2	3	5
M. Williams p	0	0	0	0	G. Davis 1b	3	0	0	0
Grace 1b	3	0	0	0	G. Wilson rf	4	0	0	1
Webster rf	3	1	1	0	Biggio c	4	1	2	0
Lancaster p	0	0	0	0	Caminiti 3b	3	1	2	0
Dawson rf	0	0	0	0	Ramirz ss	1	0	0	1
Law 3b	4	0	0	0	Yelding pr	0	1	0	0
Dunston ss	4	0	0	0	Scott p	3	0	1	0
Girardi c	4	0	1	1	Darwin p	0	0	0	0
Bielecki p	3	0	2	0	C. Reynolds ph	0	1	0	0
S. Wilson p	0	0	0	0					
McClendon lf	1	0	0	0					
Totals	**36**	**4**	**9**	**3**	**Totals**	**32**	**8**	**1**	**1**

```
CUBS            000  110  101—4
Houston         011  011  004—8
```

One out when winning run scored.

E—Scott, Biggio, Ramirez. DP—CUBS 1. LOB—CUBS 8, Houston 6. 2B—Girardi, Caminiti, Doran. 3B—Biggio. HR—Bass 2 (3), Sandberg 2 (24). SB—Bielecki (1),Webster (12). SF—Ramirez.

	IP	H	R	ER	BB	SO
CUBS						
Bielecki	5 2/3	9	4	4	3	3
S. Wilson	1	0	0	0	0	1
Lancaster L,3-1	1 1/3	1	1	1	1	2
M. Williams	1/3	1	3	3	1	1
Houston						
Scott	7	8	3	2	3	6
Darwin W, 11-3	2	1	1	1	0	1

Lancaster pitched to 1 batter in the 9th.
HBP —Young by M. Williams.
Umpires—Home, Darling; First, Marsh; Second, Rehliford; Third, Wendelstedt.
T—3:18 A—38,624.

August 21

It was great to be back at Wrigley!

I was in the outfield shagging flies before the game and a ball was hit over toward the side and, when I went after it, I saw Joe Kraemer and Dean Wilkins in uniform. I asked Darrin,"Who got sent down?" and he said Pico and Kilgus. They're both good friends of mine and I didn't even know they were going down; I didn't get a chance to wish them well and tell them they'd be back soon.

We let one get away that Monday night, 6-5. Usually when we score early we go on to win. We got three in the first on Andre's two-run double and a single by Shawon. And we were ahead, 5-1, at the end of the sixth, thanks to Ryno's homer and a triple by Mark. But our bullpen couldn't hold the lead and the Reds tied it, 5-5. In the bottom of the ninth, Shawon got caught trying to steal third and, in the 10th, Ryno was thrown out at the plate trying to score from first on Mitch Webster's double. Their run in the 10th scored on an error. It might have looked like we were feeling the pressure of being in first; I don't think that was the case—we were just in a bad streak.

Speaking of streaks, I guess it was time for mine to end. I went 0-for-4, with a walk in the first inning. I don't know how Joe DiMaggio did it for 56 straight games. With the media making a big deal out of it I had started putting pressure on myself. There's a lot of luck involved in a hitting streak—like the time I got a hit in my sixth at-bat only because the game went into extra innings. I have to say I was relieved when it was over and I could relax a little more at the plate.

It felt really good when the fans gave me a standing ovation after I had grounded to the pitcher in the 10th. During the streak I hit .338 (46-for-136) and raised my season average to .319.

August 22

Joe Kraemer got his first start on Tuesday and the Reds hit him pretty hard; by the time he left in the fourth, they had scored six runs. They went on to win it, 7-2. I was glad to get a hit in four trips; I didn't want to go on a hitless streak.

August 23

As if it wasn't bad enough that we lost our sixth in a row, 8-5, to the Reds, we almost lost Andre too. The Reds were leading, 3-2, in the sixth when Eric Davis hit a long drive to right. Andre was trying to play the ball and the wind and, just as he looked up to find the ball, his head hit the wall so hard that I could hear it. I thought for sure he had split his head open. I got the ball and threw it back and hurried over to Andre. He was conscious and talking, but he was in a lot of pain. After a few minutes, he told Zim he wanted to stay in the game. And he got a single each of his next two times up. The Reds scored three times in the ninth and so did we, but it wasn't enough.

Even after losing six games in a row, we were still in first place, one and a half ahead of the Mets, two ahead of the Expos, and two and a half ahead of the Cardinals. We knew better than to worry about how the other contenders were doing. Like somebody said, "The only team we have to watch is ourselves."

That same day the Cubs acquired Paul Assenmacher from the Braves for two players to be named later (they turned out to be Kelly Mann and Pat Gomez). We had a day off before starting a home series with Atlanta. As Zim said, we needed a day away from the park.

August 25

There was good news and bad news that Friday afternoon. It took us 12 innings, but we beat the Braves, 4-3, to end our losing streak. The bad news was that Damon had to go on the D.L. with a partial tear of the right rotator cuff. He's a great defensive catcher and he handles the pitchers well because he knows what to call. Luckily, we were rich in catchers. We had Joe Girardi and Rick Wrona—who was called up from Iowa and arrived in time to lead off the 12th with a hit and score the deciding run, when Ryno drove him in from second with a single. Assenmacher did a great job in relief. It looked as though Damon would be out for the rest of the season. Zim told the press: "No point in going over and jumping in Lake Michigan about it. We'll play musical chairs with the catching situation. I think they'll do a good job."

I got two hits and scored a run to help us get back on the winning track. I don't know how any season could ever be as exciting and as much fun as this one.

August 26

Sut got hit hard the next day and the Braves beat us, 5-3. Even though they were having a bad year, the Braves have some good young players and one of these years they're going to surprise people. We got all of our runs in the fourth off of Derek Lilliquist. But their bullpen shut us out for the last five and a third. All we could do was to come out swinging tomorrow.

August 27

I started to get a sore throat the day before and it kept me awake almost all night. I felt really weak when I got to the park and I told the trainer that I probably shouldn't play. I heard that Harry Caray couldn't understand how a sore throat could put me on the bench. It really wasn't the throat so much as the overall weakness.

It turned out to be another one of those down-to-the-last-out wins as we pulled it out, 3-2, in 10. We were behind, 2-1, in the ninth when Darrin's check-swing hit to left scored Lloyd from second with the tying run. Andre's single with two out in the 10th brought in the winning run from third. We celebrated because I think we all sensed that we were back from the losing streak of the previous week and that things were going our way again.

August 28

Houston was in town for three and we owed them for sweeping us down there. We didn't waste any time paying them back. They helped us get four runs in the first inning. I opened with a bunt single and went to second on Glenn Davis' throwing error. Ryno singled me to third. Lloyd grounded to third and Eric Yelding, after getting the force at second, tried to catch me going back to third, but I was safe. He should have gone to first for the double play and I should have run for home instead of hesitating. Mark and Andre both walked, forcing me in, and then Shawon doubled in two more and Rick Wrona hit a sacrifice fly for our fourth run. That turned out to be all we needed as Greg pitched a six-hitter for his 15th win, 6-1.

August 29

This may have been the game that proved to us that no matter what the score, our team could come back to win. We were losing, 9-0, in the sixth when we got two runs out of a walk and three singles. An inning later, I got hit by a pitch, Lloyd homered, Mark singled, went to second on a balk and scored on a single by Dwight. Now it was 9-5 and you could tell our bench was starting to sense that maybe we could do it. In the eighth, Joe singled, I reached on an error, Ryno and Lloyd singled, each driving in a run. A passed ball moved the runners to second and third. Ryno scored on Mark's single and Dwight hit a sacrifice fly to score Lloyd with the tying run. By now the crowd and our dugout were having the time of their lives. Les came in to pitch the ninth and he held them, but we failed in the bottom of the inning. Assenmacher retired them in the 10th and then we went to work. I got a walk and Ryno sacrificed me to second. Lloyd got a hit, but I had to hold up at third.

Cubs 10, Astros 9

	ab	r	h	bi		ab	r	h	bi
Young	5	0	1	0	Walton cf	4	3	0	0
Doran 2b	4	1	0	0	Sandberg 2b	5	1	3	1
Bass lf	4	1	1	0	McClendon lf	5	2	3	3
G. Davis 1b	3	2	0	0	Grace 1b	4	2	2	1
G. Wilson rf	5	0	1	0	Dawson rf	3	0	1	0
Yelding pr	0	0	0	0	D. Smith rf	2	0	2	3
Da. Smith p	0	0	0	0	Dunston ss	5	1	2	0
Caminit 3b	4	2	1	0	Ramos 3b	4	0	2	1
Biggio c	3	2	1	0	Girardi c	4	1	3	0
Ramirz ss	5	1	3	7	Bielecki p	1	0	0	0
Portugal p	3	0	0	0	Wilkins p	0	0	0	0
Meyer p	0	0	0	0	Wilkerson ph	0	0	0	0
Darwin p	0	0	0	0	Schiraldi p	0	0	0	0
Agosto p	0	0	0	0	Webster ph	1	0	0	0
Puhl rf	1	0	0	0	Sandrsn p	0	0	0	0
					Law ph	1	0	0	0
					Lancaster p	0	0	0	0
					Jackson ph	1	0	0	0
					Asnmchr p	0	0	0	0
Totals	37	9	8	7	**Totals**	40	10	18	9

Houston	020	250	000	0— 9
CUBS	000	002	340	1—10

One out when winning run scored.

E—Dunston, Portugal, Caminiti. DP—Houston 2. LOB—Houston 10, CUBS 12. 2B—Biggio, Ramirez, Dawson, Bass. HR—Ramirez (5), McClendon (11). S—Meyer, Ramos, Sandberg. SF—D. Smith.

	IP	H	R	ER	BB	SO
Houston						
Portugal	6 1/3	9	4	4	2	4
Meyer	1	4	4	2	0	0
Darwin	0	1	1	1	0	0
Agosto	2/3	1	0	0	0	0
Da. Smith L. 3-4	1 1/3	3	1	1	3	0
CUBS						
Bielecki	4	3	6	5	5	5
Wilkins	1	1	3	3	2	1
Schiraldi	1	1	0	0	0	0
Sandrsn	2	2	0	0	0	1
Lancaster	1	1	0	0	0	0
Asnmchr W, 2-3	1	0	0	0	0	1

Darwin pitched to 1 batter in the 8th.

HBP—McClendon by Portugal, Walton by Portugal. WP—Bielecki. BK—Meyer. PB—Girardi, Biggio 2.

Umpires—Home, Montague; First, Marsh; Second, Wendelstedt; Third, Darling.

T—3:46 A—25,829.

They walked Mark to fill the bases and then Dwight singled to bring me in with the winning run.

We really enjoyed that win. It was special for the fans because they stay at games where we're behind, hoping and believing that some times we'll rally and pull it out. That afternoon we did it for them. Our home attendance went over the two-million mark that day, too.

August 30

The Astros bounced back from their loss on Tuesday and beat us, 8-4, behind Mike Scott. Dwight, Ryno, and Mark each homered off of him and Mark's came after I had reached with a bunt single in the ninth so we might have scared them a little bit. Scott closed us out for the win, despite our ninth-inning noise. We had a day off the next day before starting a seven-game road trip in Atlanta. I went home a day early so I could see my family and friends in Newnan.

National League East Standings August 31, 1989	W	L	Pct.	GB
CHICAGO	75	58	.564	—
New York	72	60	.545	$2^{1/2}$
St. Louis	72	60	.545	$2^{1/2}$
Montreal	72	61	.541	3
Pittsburgh	58	74	.439	$16^{1/2}$
Philadelphia	54	79	.406	21

It's Our Division!

September 1

I got to spend time with Jonathan and take care of some business the day before. I had about 90 names to put on the pass list for this series in Atlanta. I was especially glad I came down early because the team flight came through a bad storm with bumps and lightning. Zim said there was so much lightning that you could read the paper without the cabin lights on. Too bad it didn't rain the game out. We could only get five hits and one run off of Lilliquist and we lost, 5-1. There was a lot of activity though because the day before, Calvin Schiraldi, Darrin Jackson, and a player to be named later (who turned out to be Phil Stephenson) were traded to San Diego for Luis Salazar and Marvell Wynne. Also Paul Kilgus was called up and Dean Wilkins was sent to Iowa. This was the day when

119

teams could expand the roster and the Cubs added Kevin Blankenship, Doug Dascenzo, Jeff Pico, and Gary Varsho from Iowa and Greg Smith from Charlotte.

September 2

Three Atlanta errors helped us score six runs in the first inning and we went on from there to a 10-3 win. I had a single, a double, and scored twice and it was nice to do that in front of my guests from Newnan. Rick Wrona was the big bat with a three-run homer in the first and Luis Salazar didn't waste any time getting into the swing of things with us—he had 2-for-3 with two RBIs. Greg got his 16th win and a good time was had by everybody as Zim used 16 players in the game.

September 3

We wasted two home runs by Andre as Atlanta scored three in the first and five in the fourth to beat us, 8-5. The Braves played us tough all year and we finished only 7-5 against them. I had two hits and stole home but it wasn't our day. Zim said after the game that he was looking forward to playing teams in our own division because we could control our own destiny by beating the teams that were chasing us. At that point, the Cardinals were only one-and-a-half games behind us. Our first stop was in New York for two games with the Mets.

September 4

Nobody had to tell us as we boarded the bus for Shea Stadium that we were closing in on serious business. Ryno got us off to a good start with a solo homer in the first. Then in the third we added three more when Shawon drove in Dwight and Rick Wrona singled home Mark and Andre. Sut was struggling and Zim brought in Les to start the sixth with a 4-3 lead. Les had given up only one hit over the last four innings and we came out on top, 7-3.

September 5

This was one of those games you replay in your mind. The Mets got credited with a run in the first which they shouldn't have had. With one out and the bases loaded, McReynolds hit a fly into mid-center. I caught it on the run and thought I got rid of it in good time. I had to come in at full speed, so I took an extra step to bring myself under control and then I threw it. I threw it all the way to the catcher on the fly and I thought it was there. So did Wrona. So did Zim. But the umpires didn't. They got another run in the fourth and we scored one in the sixth and then tied the game in the ninth at two apiece. Samuel singled Teufel home from second with two outs in the bottom of the ninth and the Mets won, 3-2. All we could do was put it behind us and move on to Philadelphia.

September 6

When we got to Philadelphia, Greg didn't have it and Bruce Ruffin did as the Phillies clubbed us, 9-1. To make matters worse, I hurt myself hitting the wall in the first inning. I caught Ricky Jordan's line drive, but my momentum took me into the wall and I jammed my right shoulder. That shoulder has never been perfect since I separated it in high school football. It stiffened up and hurt more as the game went on. I didn't get a hit in four trips, so it was a bad night all the way around.

September 7

The trainer worked on my shoulder and I didn't play the next day so I could rest it. That turned out all right because Doug Dascenzo took my place and hit his first major league homer, a two-run shot in the third. Mike got his 15th win in 21 decisions as we beat Ken Howell, 6-2.

For the first time in most of our lives, we all rooted for the Mets and they demolished the Cardinals, 13-1; that meant that we had a one-and-a-half-game lead over St. Louis as we flew home to meet them at Wrigley Field for three games.

September 8

It looked like we were going to beat the Cardinals just like the Mets had. We scored seven runs in the first four innings. Everybody was hitting and having fun. Ryno homered in the first and the fourth and our fans were rubbing it in to the Cardinal fans. St. Louis scored once in the second and once in the fifth, but we still led, 7-2, going into the seventh. Three singles, a double, a walk, and an error later it was 7-6. We got one back in the bottom of the seventh and then disaster struck—and fast. Guerrero homered off of Mitch with two on and then Pendleton hit one with Brunansky on and the Cardinals had come back to win, 11-8, and to move within a half game of first place.

We felt terrible. You just can't blow a lead like that in the midst of a pennant race. The clubhouse was really quiet. If we were ever going to hang our heads, it would have been then. After the final out, I just sat in the dugout and watched the Cardinals celebrate— it was like they had just won the pennant. Maybe they thought that game broke our spirit.

September 9

If there was ever a game that showed what this team was truly made of, it was played this Saturday afternoon. Our lead over the Cardinals was down to

Cubs 3, Cardinals 2

	ab	r	h	bi		ab	r	h	bi
Coleman lf	5	0	1	0	Walton cf	5	1	2	0
O. Smith ss	5	0	2	0	Sandberg 2b	3	0	0	0
M. Thompson cf	5	0	1	0	Dw. Smith lf	3	1	1	1
Guerrero 1b	3	1	1	0	Grace 1b	4	0	0	0
Pendleton 3b	3	0	0	0	Dawson rf	4	1	0	0
Brunansky rf	4	1	1	1	Law 3b	2	0	1	0
Dayley p	0	0	0	0	G. Smith pr	0	0	0	0
Oquendo 2b	4	0	1	1	Salazar 3b	2	0	2	2
T. Pena c	4	0	1	0	Dunston ss	4	0	1	0
DeLeon p	2	0	0	0	Girardi c	1	0	0	0
DiPino p	0	0	0	0	Wynne ph	1	0	0	0
Quisenberry p	0	0	0	0	Wrona c	1	0	0	0
Morris cf	1	0	0	0	Sutcliffe p	2	0	0	0
					Varsho ph	1	0	0	0
					Lancaster p	0	0	0	0
					S. Wilson p	0	0	0	0
					Pico p	0	0	0	0
					Ramos ph	0	0	0	0
					Dascenzo pr	0	0	0	0
					Assenmacher p	0	0	0	0
Totals	**36**	**2**	**8**	**2**	**Totals**	**33**	**3**	**7**	**3**

```
St. Louis      000  002  000  0—2
CUBS           100  000  010  1—3
```

E—Brunansky. LOB—St. Louis 7, CUBS 11. 2B—M.
Thompson, Salazar. 3B—Law, O. Smith. SB—M. Thompson
(25), Walton 2 (22), Brunanasky (5). S—Dw. Smith, DeLeon.

	IP	H	R	ER	BB	SO
St. Louis						
DeLeon	7	5	2	1	5	2
DiPino	1/3	0	0	0	0	1
Quisenberry	1/3	1	0	0	0	0
Dayley L,3-2	1 2/3	1	1	1	3	0
CUBS						
Sutcliffe	7	7	2	2	1	5
Lancaster	1/3	1	0	0	1	0
S. Wilson	1/3	0	0	0	0	0
Pico	1 1/3	0	0	0	0	1
Assenmacher W, 3-3	1	0	0	0	0	0

DeLeon pitched to 1 batter in the 8th.
WP—Sutcliffe. PB—T. Pena. Umpires—Home, Froemming;
First, DeMuth; Second, Rippley; Third, Tata.
Second, Hohn; Third, West.
T—3:23. A—37,633.

a half game and first place was on the line. It was a
wet and gloomy kind of day and the Cardinals had

DeLeon going against Sut. I was able to get a hit leading off our half of the first and then stole second. Two groundouts later I scored. That run held up until the top of the sixth when Guerrero, Brunansky, and Oquendo put together singles to score two runs. In the eighth, Dwight led off with a single to right and he took a wide turn at first. Brunansky has a real good arm and he never figured Dwight would risk going in a game as important as this one, so he held the ball. Instead of going back to first, Dwight challenged him and took off for second and Brunansky's throw was wide. Dwight summed up our way of playing when he said later, "You can't win if you're afraid you're going to make a mistake."

Mark fanned, but Andre grounded out to the right side, letting Dwight take third. Quisenberry was pitching now and Luis Salazar singled to left, scoring Dwight with the tying run. Jeff Pico had come on in the eighth and closed down the inning by striking out Brunansky when a hit could have scored two Cardinal runs. He got them in order in the ninth, but we couldn't get anything going against Ken Dayley. Paul Assenmacher held them in the 10th and again we had a chance to win. Andre walked with one out and scored all the way from first when Luis doubled to the right-field corner. We won, 3-2. It was our turn to celebrate. We needed that win and we outfought them to get it. It pumped us up tremendously. We knew we weren't going to fold. Scott said after the game that coming from behind to win was better for us than if we had won 100-0. He was right.

September 10

Somebody told us that it was 20 years ago this day when the Cubs fell out of first place in 1969. Not this year. Zim started Steve Wilson against the Cardinals that Sunday and he went five innings, giving up four hits, striking out 10, and still left trailing, 1-0. We didn't score until the bottom of the sixth when Dwight homered with Ryno on base. We got another in the seventh when Luis doubled and I singled him home. In the eighth Shawon drove Andre home with our final run. Meanwhile, Scott, Paul, and Mitch added eight more strikeouts in the last four innings to give our pitchers 18 for the game. Our 4-1 win put us two and a half ahead of the Cardinals and four games ahead of Montreal. But there was no time to rest because next we had the Expos at Wrigley for three games and Montreal was fighting for its life in the pennant race.

September 11

We beat Mark Langston in the first game of the Montreal series and once again it was the whole team that did it. No one was carrying this team—we were all doing our part. Greg won his 17th game, with help from Les and Mitch. Shawon got us going with a two-run triple in the second and the Expos got two in the fourth to tie. We went ahead with one run in the fifth when Luis walked with the bases loaded to force in Shawon. Marquis Grissom homered in the Expo sixth and we were tied again. Then, in the seventh, Rick Wrona doubled and went to third on an error. My single brought him home with what proved to be the winning run. But the game didn't end without some more excitement.

There were two out and two on when Zim called in Mitch to relieve Les. While he was warming up, Lloyd walked over to the mound from first base, where he was playing in place of Mark. Lloyd suggested that they try to pick off Jeff Huson, the pinch runner at first. Back in April Mitch had picked Carmelo Martinez off of second to end the game. This time he told Lloyd, "Let's get him on the second pitch." After Mitch threw ball one, Lloyd broke from behind Huson as Mitch went into his motion. Mitch had to hold up a little to give his first baseman time to reach the bag, so the ball came in on a bounce. It didn't matter; Huson was caught and the game was over: Cubs 4, Expos 3.

I don't care how good a team is, in baseball you have to get breaks now and then to win. Talent at the major league level is pretty even on at least three or four teams in a division, so there are a lot of other things that determine who is going to win. A lot of things happened right for us this season and we played aggressively enough to make them happen—to force other teams to make mistakes. Even so, there is an element in baseball that no statistic can capture and it is just plain old luck.

September 12

We won another game this night, thanks to a combination of great pitching by Mike Bielecki, a break in the form of a passed ball by Nelson Santovenia that allowed Vance to score in the fourth, and a solo homer by Ryno in the eighth that insured our 2-0 win. Mike gave up only two hits and pitched his third shutout of the season to bring his record to 16-6. He is a great example of how hard work and perseverance pay off. Ryno's home run was his 30th of the year and that's the first time that's been done by a second baseman in 10 years. Bobby Grich of the Angels was the last one to do it. Ryno is deceptive. He doesn't have a big home run cut and he doesn't really try to hit homers. But his swing is so compact and so strong that the balls just get launched off his bat.

September 13

We completed the three-game sweep of the Expos and even their manager admitted that we had knocked them out of the race. It was a good game as Scott and Les combined to hold the Expos to one run on nine hits. Meanwhile, we got some help from the Expos. In the second, Kevin Gross made a mental mistake that allowed Mark to get back to second base when he had been trapped between second and third. We went on to get a run out of two fielder's choices, a wild pitch, and a single by Joe Girardi. That made up for a lapse on my part in the first. I had led off with a bunt hit with a two-strike count and then I stole second. I had a big lead and Gross tried to pick me off. I didn't see that the throw had gone through to center field because I was diving back into second. By the time I got up and took off for third, Dave Martinez had the ball and he threw me out.

In the fifth, Andre brought Ryno in from second with a single to right and we were up, 2-0. They got a rally started in the sixth. Hubie Brooks was on third and Foley on first with one out when Ed Fitzgerald lined one into center. Even though my shoulder had been bothering me, I couldn't let it stop me from playing all out. If you start worrying about that sort of thing, you're going to hold back and things are going to happen that shouldn't happen. The wind was blowing in, so I knew I had to charge the ball as fast as I could and then dive to make the catch. I guess Brooks didn't think I'd get it because he didn't tag up. By the time he did get back to third, I had caught the ball and was back on my feet and ready to throw him out if he tried to run. We added another run in the eighth when Shawon singled Mark home from second. It finished, 3-1.

We were glad to see Montreal drop out of the race. Andre had said that he thought they were the team to beat and now we'd done just that. The mood of the team was positive but not overconfident. There was a lot of work to be done yet. But for the moment we were where we needed to be. We were off to Pittsburgh for two games.

September 15

We won our sixth straight, thanks to Rick's pitching and Shawon's first major league grand slam. The final score was 7-2. Ever since that fan started showing up with the Shawon-O-Meter, he'd been hitting like a man on a mission. We were five-and-a-half games ahead of the Mets right now. As Zim said, we weren't celebrating, but we didn't think the worst was going to happen either.

September 16

Greg Maddux made a rare fielding mistake and it ended up costing three unearned runs and we lost the next day, 8-6. The Pirates led, 3-0, at the end of one; we led, 4-3, at the end of three; then they scored five and we came back with two in the ninth. The Mets and Cardinals lost, too, so at least we didn't slip in our lead.

September 17

Doug Drabek shut us out—even though we had eight hits—and Mike Bielecki lost a tough one, 2-0. We were trying to win every game because we didn't want to back into this championship. Mike's record went to 16-7 and we figured that, if he kept pitching that well, we'd win nine out of 10 for him. Drabek had been tough on us all year—every pitch was a slider or curveball. He doesn't throw very many fastballs and, if he does, he throws them high to try to get you to chase them. He is a fine pitcher.

Mike Bielecki was a big surprise to lots of people.

He said that pitching in winter ball helped him a lot. Not only did he work on a new pitch, he said that when the fans were throwing fireworks at you, you just wanted to get three outs and get back to the dugout.

Given that we lost two of three to the Pirates, we were more than happy to leave Pittsburgh and to head home to Wrigley to face the Mets.

We had been reading in the paper that Jim Frey said that he'd been with some good teams and some bad teams, but that our team was the best because nobody gave us a chance to win and he would have taken .500 at the beginning of the season. Zim told the press that no matter whether we won the division or not, he was proud of this team and we'd had a great season. We understood what they were saying, but we didn't look at it like that—we wanted to win every game and there was no way we would accept not winning the division.

September 18
The Mets came in five-and-a-half games behind and they knew that they needed to win both games against us to have a chance. They got off to a good start with three runs off of Paul Kilgus in the first three innings, two of them being home runs by Jefferies and Strawberry. With Viola pitching, they carried a 3-0 lead into the bottom of the fifth. Viola is a finesse pitcher and we wanted to get to him relatively early. My hamstring had been hurting for three or four days, but I didn't say anything because I wanted to play. In the fifth I hit a grounder back up the middle to Jefferies and I had to go as hard as I could to beat it out. I was safe, but I reinjured my leg.

I stayed in long enough to score after Ryno walked and Mark singled. Then Jefferies made an error and Luis homered and we had a 4-3 lead. We added two more in the sixth. We were leading, 6-4, in the bottom of the eighth when we scored four times—three on Mitch Williams' first career hit—a home run with two on. We were giving him a lot of kidding, but he got us back for that by scaring us in the ninth. The Mets scored twice and had the bases loaded with Darryl Strawberry the tying run at the plate. We didn't breathe easy until Mitch struck out Strawberry to end the game. The final score was 10-6.

The win, for all practical purposes, left only St. Louis with an outside chance to catch us. We were happy, but not ready to celebrate yet.

September 19

I didn't dress for the Tuesday game with New York because I was getting treatment for my hamstring. Marvell Wynne played center and Shawon led off in my absence. My leg hurt, but not being able to play hurt even more. Yet I knew that, if I gave my leg a rest then, I could be back before the end of the season and be ready for the playoffs.

The Mets beat us, 5-2, thanks to a three-run homer by Gary Carter off of Steve Wilson. Our lead over St. Louis was now four games and people were starting to say that the whole season would come down to the final series between us and the Cardinals in St. Louis. We were hoping that we'd clinch it by then.

September 20

The Phillies came to town and, by beating us, 9-8, cut our lead over the Cardinals to three games. Nobody was panicking but we knew we had to win some games in order to control our destiny. Zim had a closed meeting after the game and he basically just told us to relax, stay loose, and play our game. He knew that the game that day was not typical and didn't signal a choke. Our pitching had been there all year when we needed it and we figured it would be back.

September 21

Greg Maddux pitched a six-hitter for his seventh complete game and we clobbered the Phillies, 9-1. Andre hit his 19th homer and eight of our starting lineup had at least two hits each. The Cards lost and our lead was back up to four.

September 22

Pittsburgh threw Doug Drabek at us on Friday and we hit him for four runs while Mike was holding the Pirates to two and that reduced the magic number to five. Mitch got his 35th save of the season. The Cardinals won, so we remained four ahead. Optimistically, the Cubs' ticket lottery for the playoffs began that day.

September 23

It was another exciting game on Saturday and another great win for us. We won it on a hit by Mitch Webster, scoring Curtis Wilkerson, to break a 2-2 tie in the bottom of the ninth. Paul Kilgus and Les Lancaster held the Pirates to two runs on six hits and kept us in it until we could score and win, 3-2. We knew we were not going to fold now, despite the fact the Frank DiPino was telling the press that Zim would choke. We'd take care of DiPino if he faced us in St. Louis.

September 24

This was our last home game of the year and we all really wanted to win it for our fans. They had been loyal and supportive and all of us really wanted to play hard and well for them. If the fans ever wonder whether we hear them, I can tell you we do—and the opposing team hears them too—and there is a subtle but real surge that happens when the crowd gets into the game. Happily we beat the Pirates, 4-2, behind Steve Wilson, Dean Wilkins, and Jeff Pico.

After the game, we went out to congratulate Jeff and then headed into the clubhouse. The fans refused to leave—they stayed in the park and cheered. We had the TV on in the clubhouse and the broadcasters were saying that they wished we'd go back out onto the field like the Cubs did in 1984 after the final home game. The difference was that in 1984 the team had already clinched the division—our magic number was still three. Vance and Mark went back into the dugout to take a look and then they came back and said we really should go out to take a bow so as to thank our fans for their great support. Mark was the first one out of the dugout and the fans went wild when they saw him and as the rest of us followed. We circled the field, waving to the crowd; I took special note of the fans in the center-field bleachers who had supported me all season. It was a really moving experience for all of us—it was one of the most awesome feelings I've ever had. I won't ever forget it.

Next we were going on the road for our last six games.

Cubs 4, Pirates 2

	ab	r	h	bi		ab	r	h	bi
Bonds lf	4	0	0	0	Wynne cf	4	2	2	0
Bell ss	4	0	1	0	Sandberg 2b	4	1	2	1
King 3b	3	0	0	0	D. Smith lf	4	0	2	2
Taylor p	0	0	0	0	Grace 1b	4	0	0	0
Bonilla 1b	3	2	1	1	Dawson rf	4	0	2	0
R. Reynolds rf	3	0	2	0	Salazar 3b	4	0	2	0
VanSlyke cf	3	0	0	0	Assenmacher p	0	0	0	0
Lind 2b	4	0	1	1	Pico p	0	0	0	0
Bilardello c	1	0	0	0	Ramos ss	3	1	2	0
LaValliere c	1	0	0	0	Girardi c	2	0	1	1
Redus ph	0	0	0	0	S. Wilson p	2	0	0	0
Distefano ph	1	0	0	0	Wilkins p	1	0	0	0
J. Robinson p	1	0	0	0	M. Williams p	0	0	0	0
B. Hatcher ph	1	0	0	0	Law 3b	0	0	0	0
Patterson p	0	0	0	0					
R. Reed p	0	0	0	0					
Cangelosi cf	2	0	1	0					
Totals	**31**	**2**	**6**	**2**	**Totals**	**32**	**4**	**1**	**3**

```
Pittsburgh          000  100  001—2
CUBS                111  010  00x—4
```

E—J. Robinson 2, Ramos, LaValliere. DP—Pittsburgh 4, CUBS 1. LOB—Pittsburgh 7, CUBS 5. 2B— Sandberg, R. Reynolds, Lind. 3B—Ramos. HR—Bonilla (24). SB—Wynne (6). S—Bilardello.

	IP	H	R	ER	BB	SO
Pittsburgh						
J. Robinson L, 7-12	4	6	3	2	1	4
Patterson	1	2	1	1	0	0
R. Reed	2	2	0	0	0	2
Taylor	1	3	0	0	0	0
CUBS						
S. Wilson W, 6-4	5	3	1	1	2	4
Wilkins	3	2	0	0	0	4
M. Williams	0	0	1	1	2	0
Assenmacher	1/3	1	0	0	0	1
Pico S, 1	2/3	0	0	0	0	1

S. Wilson pitched to 1 batter in the 6th. M. Williams pitched to 2 batters in the 9th.
WP—J. Robinson.
Umpires—Home, Kibler; First, Davis; Second, Quick; Third, Gregg.
T—2:43 A—37,904.

September 25

It took a run in the ninth to tie us and another in the 10th to beat us as we lost to the Expos, 4-3. Andre had a two-homer game, which usually means he's on a hot streak, and the second one was inside the park. It was the 10th time in his career he had 20 or more home runs in a season. Although we lost, the Pirates beat the Cardinals to reduce the magic number to two. We had worked long and hard to get where we were; we could wait another day or so to celebrate.

Meanwhile, we heard that the playoff ticket lottery had 27 million calls over the weekend! Too bad we couldn't have everybody there for a game.

September 26

Like most of our games this season, this one went right down to the final inning before being decided. Rick Wrona tripled, scoring Shawon with a run in the second. In the sixth, Ryno scored on Mark's clutch hit. But the Expos scored twice in the bottom of the sixth to tie it. Just about then the scoreboard showed that once again the Pirates had knocked off the Cardinals. That meant the magic number was down to one and we knew that this was a great chance to get it done. With two outs in the eighth, Ryno singled off of Dennis Martinez. Dwight was up next and he had had a hot bat for the last week or so. He was 12 for his last 19. You could tell he was going to get a hit. When his single into right got away from Hubie Brooks, Ryno came all the way around to score. Greg pitched into the ninth and, when the Expos got a runner on, Zim brought in Mitch to close out. They got the tying run to third with two out and pinch hitter Mike Fitzgerald up. He usually hits well against us, but Mitch let it fly and struck him out. We were the champions of the Eastern Division, the first team to clinch a title that year! And we won that night the way we won all year—good pitching, good defense, and aggressive baserunning.

Cubs 3, Montreal 2								
	ab	r	h	bi		ab	r	h	bi
Wynne cf	4	0	0	0	Raines lf	4	0	1	0
Sandberg 2b	4	2	2	0	Grissom cf	4	1	1	0
D. Smith lf	4	0	3	1	Galarraga 1b	4	1	1	0
Dascenzo lf	0	0	0	0	Brooks rf	4	0	1	1
Grace 1b	3	0	1	0	Wallach 3b	4	0	0	0
Dawson rf	4	0	0	0	Foley 2b	3	0	2	0
Salazar 3b	3	0	0	0	O. Nixon pr	0	0	0	0
Dunston ss	4	1	1	0	Santovenia c	2	0	1	1
Wrona c	4	0	1	1	Owen ss	3	0	0	0
Girardi c	0	0	0	0	W. Johnson ph	1	0	0	0
G. Maddux p	3	0	0	0	D. Martinez p	2	0	0	0
M. Williams p	0	0	0	0	Fitzgerald ph	1	0	0	0
Totals	**33**	**3**	**8**	**2**	**Totals**	**32**	**2**	**7**	**2**

```
CUBS              010  001  010—3
Montreal          000  002  000—2
```
E—Salazar, Brooks. DP—Montreal 2. LOB—
CUBS 5, Montreal 7. 2B—Raines, Sandberg. 3B—Wrona.
SB—Raines (40), O. Nixon (37). S—D. Martinez,
Santovenia. SF—Santovenia.

	IP	H	R	ER	BB	SO
CUBS						
G. Maddux W, 19-12	8 1/3	7	2	2	1	6
M. Williams S, 36	2/3	0	0	0	0	1
Montreal						
D. Martinez L, 16-7	9	8	3	2	2	7

Umpires—Home, Rennert; First, Runge;
Second, Brocklander; Third, Engel.
T—2:55 A—11,615.

Even though you feel sure you're going to win it, there's nothing like the moment when it actually happens—the whole season kind of comes back to you and you look around at the joy on the faces of everybody who has been through it all together. We didn't do it the easy way. We had to scratch and fight and rally and regroup all season long. We picked each other up and kept going, even when people thought we were through. We'd come back from a losing streak and win not just one, but two or three or four in a row to get back on track. And it wasn't just eight regulars, six pitchers, and an unusual bench. Everybody in our clubhouse had good memories to share with his children and grandchildren about how he helped this team to win. That's the kind of emotion and feeling that came out in our clubhouse after the game. People were pouring champagne all over each other and hugging and high-fiving and laughing and just plain enjoying every minute of it all.

We had a television in the clubhouse so that we could see the celebration around Wrigley Field. We all wished we could have been home with our fans. A reporter asked Ryno about 1984 and he said, "That was a long time ago. This beats everything!"

September 27

We took the season series from the Expos 10 games to eight by beating them, 7-2, behind Mike and Jeff. It was Mike's 18th win against seven losses. We had a 7-0 lead in the ninth and Zim said, "It's been so long since we had a seven-run lead I didn't know how to act." It really did seem that way. Zim was giving everybody a chance to play and to enjoy being part of the tune-up for the playoffs.

September 28

We came to St. Louis for our final series of the regular season and, instead of having to battle them in a do-or-die matchup, we could simply play them a few games of baseball. My hamstring was improved enough that I got to play in the game and I beat out an RBI infield single in the fifth. My timing was a little rusty and I hoped I could play in the last couple of games so that I could work on it. The Cardinals scored once in the seventh and twice in the eighth to beat us, 7-5.

September 30

Not only did we beat the Cardinals on Saturday,

6-4, but Ryne Sandberg tied the major league record of 89 consecutive errorless games by a second base- man set by Manny Trillo seven years ago. Zim had only used him for an inning or two in the last four games and, as he said, that doesn't make it any less a record for Ryno because he's played almost every inning of every game for years and he deserved the record. That's the kind of thing that makes us appreciate Zim. In fact, several of the guys were talking up beating the Cardinals so maybe we could knock them down to third place and cost DiPino second-place money for the stuff he said about Zim. As it turned out, we did get a run off of DiPino in a third of an inning that day.

I went 0-for-3; my timing was getting a little better and I saw the ball better in this game. I still wasn't ready to run full out; I had to favor my leg a little bit until I was sure it wouldn't pop on me.

Zim used 22 players that afternoon. Mitch had a chance to tie the Cub saves record, but he couldn't hold our 4-1 lead. We had to score two in the ninth, but that was good because it reminded us that since mid-July we'd been pretty good at winning games in our last at-bat.

October 1

We won our final game, 5-1. Ryno set the major league record at 90, Sut pitched six innings and allowed only one run to get his 16th win, and DiPino and his teammates finished third instead of second. Not bad for a day's work. After all the tension of a great race, we ended up six full games ahead of the second-place Mets.

I went hitless in four tries, which was a disap- pointment because I was hoping to finish closer to .300. Still, the Cubs had the highest team batting average in the league and we were the only team with three hitters in the top 10: Mark at .314, me at .293, and Ryno at .290. Dwight didn't have enough at-bats to qualify for the league statistics, but he did have the highest average of a Cub rookie since 1922—.324.

Now it was time to go home and use the next couple of days to get ready for the Giants. It was a great flight back to Chicago. We had come a long way from Mesa, Arizona and we didn't believe anything was going to stop us now.

National League East Final Standings								
1989								
	W	L	PCT.	GB	HOME	ROAD	Vs. EAST	Vs. WEST
CHICAGO	93	69	.574	—	48-33	45-36	53-37	40-32
New York	87	75	.537	6	51-30	36-45	48-42	39-33
St. Louis	86	76	.531	7	46-35	40-41	44-46	42-30
Montreal	81	81	.500	12	44-37	37-44	42-48	39-33
Pittsburgh	74	88	.457	19	39-42	35-46	43-47	31-41
Philadelphia	67	95	.414	26	38-42	29-33	40-50	27-45

10 The Playoffs

Even though you know a playoff game is something very special, you really have to approach it like any other game. You try not to get too high—you just want to go out there and do the things you have been doing all year. But it's tough not to get really pumped up when there is such an electric atmosphere. It seems as if there are hundreds of people from the press—almost everybody seems to have a notebook, microphone, or tape recorder in hand.

We had Monday off—even if it wasn't really a day of rest. As the season progressed, I found out first-hand about the hundreds of requests and invitations that keep your phone ringing. I tried all year to accommodate as many radio phone interviews as I could because doing that kind of thing goes with the territory. Remember, only a year ago I was playing at Pittsfield and that was all the peace and quiet anyone could need!

We had a workout at Wrigley on Tuesday. My

139

hamstring felt just about back to normal. I knew one thing: the whole season had come down to this series and I was not going to hold back. It seemed like the time dragged on forever until it was time to leave for the ball park.

October 4

I think most of us young players took our cue from our teammates who had been in a playoff before; guys such as Ryno, Andre, Sut, and Scott were loose and laughing and enjoying it all. We knew the Giants were a good team, but we also knew that we had played them even all year. We split 12 games, splitting six games at Candlestick and six at Wrigley. On the season we were 93-69 and they were 92-70.

When we went out for the introductions and the National Anthem, I have to admit it was a lot like Opening Day. I really enjoyed the introduction because the camera was right there, focused up close on each player, so you could say "hi" to Mom. Having been on the other side of the TV screen during many playoffs and World Series games, it was hard to believe that for a short moment I was the focus of all those viewers.

About five minutes after the game started, I was wishing we could say "that was just practice" and start over. Greg Maddux had willingly given up a chance to win his 20th game of the year in the second-to-last game of the season. He said it would be better for the team if he rested and saved his strength for the playoffs. But that Wednesday night he just didn't have it. I saw later on a tape of the game that the camera caught Greg sort of shaking his head when he was completing his warmups on the sideline. Pitchers know when they have it and when they don't. But even if you don't think you've got your best stuff, you go ahead and pitch because sometimes you pick up your rhythm and stuff as the game goes on.

```
                    Giants 11, Cubs 3
                 ab  r  h  bi                   ab  r  h  bi
Butler cf         4  2  1  0    Walton cf        4  0  1  0
Thompson 2b       4  1  1  0    Wilson p         0  0  0  0
Clark 1b          4  4  4  6    Ramos            1  0  0  0
Mitchell lf       5  2  2  3    Sandberg 2b      5  2  3  1
M. Williams 3b    4  0  1  2    Smith lf         4  0  0  0
Kennedy c         4  0  1  0    Grace 1b         4  1  3  2
Manwaring c       1  0  0  0    Dawson rf        3  0  0  0
Sheridan rf       4  1  2  0    Salazar 3b       4  0  2  0
Maldonado rf      1  0  0  0    Dunston ss       4  0  0  0
Uribe ss          4  1  1  0    Wrona c          4  0  0  0
Garrelts p        3  0  0  0    Maddux p         1  0  0  0
Bathe c           1  0  0  0    Law              1  0  0  0
Brantley p        0  0  0  0    Kilgus p         0  0  0  0
Hammaker p        0  0  0  0    Wynne cf         1  0  0  0
                               McClendon        1  0  1  0
Totals          39 11 13 11    Totals          37  3 10  3
```

San Francisco	301	400	030 —11
CUBS	201	000	000 — 3

LOB—Giants 6, CUBS 8. 2B—Clark, M. Williams, Sandberg. 3B—Sheridan, Salazar. HR—Clark 2, Mitchell, Sandberg, Grace. SB—Grace 1, Uribe 1. S—Thompson. HBP—M. Williams by Maddux. WP—Wilson. PB—Wrona.

	IP	H	R	ER	BB	SO
San Francisco						
Garrelts W, 1-0	7	8	3	3	1	6
Brantley	1	1	0	0	0	1
Hammaker	1	1	0	0	0	0
CUBS						
Maddux L, 0-1	4	8	8	8	1	3
Kilgus	3	4	0	0	1	1
Wilson	2	1	3	0	1	2

Umpires—Home, Harvey; First, Froemming; Second, Tata; Third, Quick; Left, Williams; Right, Marsh.
T—2:51. A-39,195.

I know it wasn't a matter of Greg being nervous or scared. He doesn't know what scared is. I heard that in his first major league game he threw inside to Dave Parker and Parker let Greg know he didn't like it—so then Greg did it again. A year later, he gave up a victory by retaliating against the Padres after Eric Show had beaned Andre Dawson. He got kicked out of the game, needing only one more out to complete five innings and qualify for the win. It was more important that he let his teammates know he'd protect them. That's a guy you want to have on the mound in tough games.

Unfortunately, before we even knew it, the Giants had scored three runs in the first inning on four hits. Giants starter, Scott Garrelts, isn't someone you normally beat if he gets a good lead on you. He was 14-5 with a 2.28 ERA for the season.

After I grounded out leading off our half of the first, Ryno doubled. Dwight struck out. Then Mark hit a home run to left-center and suddenly we were back in the game. Will Clark, who had doubled in the first, homered in the third to put the Giants ahead, 4-2, but Ryno answered with a homer in the bottom of the third and, once again, it looked like we were going to hang in until we squeezed a run home to win it.

But it was the Giants' night. In the fourth, after two singles, a strikeout and a walk loaded the bases. Thompson struck out. Zim went out to talk to Greg and Rick Wrona about how they planned to pitch to Clark. Greg wanted it to go on the inside corner, but he got it over the plate and Clark hit a grandslam to right. Now the Giants led, 8-3, and they got three more in the eighth when Kevin Mitchell lined one over the wall in left for an 11-3 Giant win.

I got a single off of Garrelts in the seventh, but it didn't lead anywhere. We just didn't play well that night, but as Zim said, "This isn't a one-game playoff. The sun will be up tomorrow. There's another game and we'll be here to play in it."

October 5

Rick Reuschel obviously knows how to pitch at Wrigley Field and he likes to face the Cubs. His lifetime record against us is 11-3 with a 1.66 ERA. He'd been tough on us all season. Even though he was 1-1 against us, he had allowed us only three runs in $16^{1/3}$ innings.

Cubs 9, Giants 5

	ab	r	h	bi		ab	r	h	bi
Butler cf	4	0	0	0	Walton cf	4	2	3	1
Thompson 2b	4	1	1	1	Sandberg 2b	3	2	1	1
Clark 1b	4	1	1	0	Smith lf	4	1	1	0
Mitchell lf	4	2	3	2	Grace 1b	4	1	3	4
M. Williams 3b	4	1	2	2	Dawson rf	4	0	0	0
Kennedy c	2	0	1	0	Salazar 3b	3	1	1	1
Bathe	0	0	0	0	Lancaster p	1	0	0	0
Oberkfell 3b	2	0	0	0	Dunston ss	3	1	1	0
Bedrosian p	0	0	0	0	Girardi c	3	1	0	0
Sheridan rf	3	0	0	0	Bielecki p	2	0	1	2
Lefferts p	0	0	0	0	Assenmacher p	0	0	0	0
Brantley p	0	0	0	0	Law 3b	2	0	0	0
Litton 3b	1	0	1	0					
Uribe ss	2	0	1	0					
Riles	1	0	0	0					
Manwaring c	1	0	0	0					
Reuschel p	0	0	0	0					
Downs p	1	0	0	0					
Nixon rf	2	0	0	0					
Totals	35	5	10	5	**Totals**	33	9	11	9

```
San Francisco        000  200  021  —5
CUBS                 600  003  00x  —9
```

DP—Giants 2. LOB—Giants 7, CUBS 8. 2B—Kennedy, Smith, Grace 2. 3B—Sandberg. HR—Thompson, Mitchell, M. Williams. SB—Dunston 1. S—Downs. PB—Manwaring.

	IP	H	R	ER	BB	SO
San Francisco						
Reuschel L,0-1	2/3	5	5	5	0	1
Downs	4 2/3	5	3	3	5	5
Lefferts	2/3	1	1	1	2	1
Brantley	1	0	0	0	1	1
Bedrosian	1	0	0	0	1	1
CUBS						
Bielecki	4 2/3	4	2	2	3	3
Assenmacher	1/3	2	0	0	0	0
Lancaster W, 1-0	4	4	3	3	0	2

T—3:08, A—39,195

But it didn't take us long to get to him in Game Two. It was just like we had done all year—we'd bounce back from a big loss with a big win and usually scored early in doing so. That night I hit Reuschel's first pitch into left for a single. Ryno hit his next pitch for a triple with the hit-and-run on. Dwight lined to first, but then Mark doubled, Andre fanned, and Luis singled to drive in Mark. Next, Shawon singled and that was all for Reuschel. The crowd, which had been going crazy over our early hitting show, gave "Big Daddy" a great ovation when he left the mound, since he had been a favorite when he played for the Cubs. Cub fans are definitely a class act.

Kelly Downs came in and walked Joe Girardi to load the bases. Downs went to 3-and-1 on Mike and had to put one down the middle; Mike not only hit it, he drove it up the middle for a two-run single. Then I got my second hit of the inning and Joe scored. By the time Dwight grounded out, we had sent up 12 batters, scored six runs on seven hits, and left the bases loaded.

In the third, Robby Thompson hit a line drive to deep center. It was one of those tough ones, right over my head. I went back and jumped as high as I could and caught it. I didn't hit the wall this time, but my momentum carried me right to the vines.

The Giants didn't score until the fourth when Clark singled and Mitchell homered to make it 6-2. In the fifth with Uribe on second and two outs, Mike walked Thompson after being ahead of him 1-and-2. Clark was up next and the wind was blowing out. Zim decided to bring in Assenmacher and he got Clark to ground out on his first pitch. Mike didn't blame Zim for taking him out—he said he should have gotten Thompson.

The Giants threatened again in the sixth, but Les

came in and got three hitters in a row, stranding two runners. In our sixth I got my third hit. Ryno and Dwight walked and then Mark drove all three of us home with a double to right. That made it 9-2. The Giants scored two in the eighth on a homer by Matt Williams and one in the ninth when Thompson homered—they are like us because they just don't give up—but we held it at 9-5 and evened the series.

After the game Mark gave me credit for setting the stage by getting a hit on the first pitch. I have to be the one to get us started—that's my job as leadoff hitter. But I'll take a compliment from a guy who's hitting .750 any day.

Everyone could see that Will Clark had been talking to our baserunners. When guys do that, they might be trying to get your mind off the game and trying to set up a pickoff play. When I singled in the first, he said something like, "Are you swinging good?" I said one word back to him and took my lead. I didn't want to have a conversation with him.

Andre was having a really tough series so far. He was hitless in seven trips. I knew that he was in tremendous pain with his knee and it couldn't help but distract him. But he wanted to play and he felt he could help us. Zim wasn't going to sit him down—he figured, as we did, that you never could tell when Andre would come out of it and hit a three-run homer when we needed it most.

October 7

Game Three was one we should have won but didn't. It was unusually still and warm in Candlestick Park and we felt good coming in with our win in Game Two. We started out with two runs in the first off of Mike LaCoss. Ryno and Dwight singled and later scored on Andre's single to center. But the Giants came back with three against Sut in the first,

Giants 5, Cubs 4

	ab	r	h	bi		ab	r	h	bi
Butler cf	4	2	2	0	Walton cf	5	0	0	0
Thompson 2b	4	2	2	2	Sandberg	3	1	1	1
Clark 1b	4	0	2	0	Smith lf	5	1	1	0
Mitchell lf	3	1	1	0	Grace 1b	3	0	2	0
M. Williams 3b	4	0	0	1	Dawson rf	4	0	1	2
Kennedy c	3	0	0	0	Salazar 3b	4	0	1	0
Maldonado rf	2	0	0	1	Wilkerson 3b	0	0	0	0
Robinson p	0	0	0	0	Dunston ss	4	1	2	0
Lefferts p	0	0	0	0	Girardi c	2	0	1	0
Oberkfell	1	0	0	0	Wynne	0	0	0	0
Bedrosian p	0	0	0	0	McClendon c	1	0	0	0
Uribe ss	4	0	1	1	Sutcliffe p	2	0	1	0
LaCoss p	1	0	0	0	Maddux	0	1	0	0
Brantley p	0	0	0	0	Assenmacher p	0	0	0	0
Nixon rf	1	0	0	0	Lancaster p	0	0	0	0
Sheridan rf	0	0	0	0	Webster	1	0	0	0
Totals	**31**	**5**	**8**	**5**	**Totals**	**34**	**4**	**10**	**3**

```
CUBS              200  100  100  —4
San Francisco     300  000  20x  —5
```

E—LaCoss, Uribe, Nixon.　DP—CUBS 1, Giants 2.
LOB— CUBS 8, Giants 6.　2B—Grace, Sutcliffe.　HR—Clark.
S—Sutcliffe, Girardi.　SF— Sandberg.

	IP	H	R	ER	BB	SO
CUBS						
Sutcliffe	6	5	3	3	4	2
Assenmacher	1/3	1	1	1	0	0
Lancaster L, 1-1	1 2/3	2	1	1	0	1
San Francisco						
LaCoss	3	7	3	3	0	2
Brantley	3	0	0	0	1	1
Robinson W,1-0	1 2/3	3	1	0	0	0
Lefferts	1/3	0	0	0	0	0
Bedrosian S,1	1	0	0	0	1	0

thanks to a couple of breaks and a bases-loaded walk. In the second, Joe Girardi was in scoring position, but I couldn't get him home. Mark doubled with two out in the third, but was stranded. We finally caught them in the fourth when Luis and Shawon opened with singles and LaCoss misplayed Joe's sacrifice. But Sut grounded into a home-to-first double play. Jeff Brantley threw a wild pitch, scoring Shawon. I flied out to left, leaving Joe at third. At least we had tied them at three. It stayed that way until the seventh when we took the lead. Sut led off with a double and, when I lined out to Clark, he tried to double Sut off, but Uribe missed the throw, allowing him to get to third. Sut strained a muscle in the process, so Greg went in to run for him and scored on Ryno's sacrifice fly.

Paul Assenmacher relieved and Donnell Nixon hit a shot to left on which Dwight made a great catch. Then Butler singled and, when the count on Robby Thompson was 0-and-1, Zim brought in Les. Thompson hit his second pitch, a sinker, over the leftfield wall and the Giants had a 5-4 lead.

In the eighth, it looked like we'd get them back. Mark led off with his second hit. When Andre hit a fly to deep left, Mark tagged up and took off for second. Mitchell's throw barely beat him there. Then Luis reached on an error and Shawon singled, but Lloyd flied out to end the inning. Our last chance came when Ryno walked with two out in the ninth, but Dwight flew out and the game was over.

There was all kind of second-guessing after the game. But the moves, such as Zim changing pitchers and Mark trying to surprise them, are the kinds of things that got us where we were. We left too many people in scoring position that night, but we were determined to come back. This team didn't know the meaning of the word "quit."

October 8

Game Four was another battle that we needed to win, should have won, and didn't. We scored in the first when Ryno doubled and Dwight singled. Mark got Ryno home with a sacrifice fly. Again the Giants came right back to tie us, 1-1, at the end of one. In the second Luis hit a long homer to center to put us up, 2-1. It stayed that way until Matt Williams singled home two runs in the third. Greg gave up

Giants 6, Cubs 4

	ab	r	h	bi		ab	r	h	bi
Butler cf	4	1	1	0	Walton cf	5	1	2	0
Thompson 2b	3	1	1	0	Sandberg 2b	5	1	2	0
Clark 1b	4	2	3	0	Smith lf	2	0	1	0
Mitchell lf	3	0	0	1	McClendon lf-c	1	0	1	0
M. Williams 3b	4	1	2	4	Grace 1b	3	1	1	2
Kennedy c	4	0	1	0	Dawson rf	5	0	1	1
Nixon	0	0	0	0	Salazar 3b	4	1	2	1
Manwaring c	0	0	0	0	Dunston ss	4	0	2	0
Sheridan rf	4	0	0	0	Wrona c	1	0	0	0
Uribe ss	4	1	1	0	Wynne	1	0	0	0
Garrelts p	1	0	0	0	Girardi c	2	0	0	0
Downs p	2	0	0	0	M. Williams p	0	0	0	0
Bedrosian p	0	0	0	0	Maddux p	2	0	0	0
					Wilson p	0	0	0	0
					Wilkerson	1	0	0	0
					Sanderson p	0	0	0	0
					Webster lf	1	0	0	0
Totals	**33**	**6**	**9**	**5**	**Totals**	**37**	**4**	**12**	**4**

```
CUBS            110  020  000 —4
San Francisco   102  1209 00x —6
```

E—Uribe, Maddux. DP—Giants 1. LOB—CUBS 10, Giants 6. 2B—Clark 2, Uribe, Sandberg, Dawson. 3B—Grace. HR—M. Williams, Salazar. SB—Smith 1, Nixon 1. SF—Grace. WP—Garrelts, Maddux.

	IP	H	R	ER	BB	SO
CUBS						
Maddux	$3^{1/3}$	5	4	3	3	2
Wilson L, 0-1	$1^{2/3}$	2	2	2	0	2
Sanderson	2	2	0	0	0	1
M. Williams	1	0	0	0	0	2
San Francisco						
Garrelts	$4^{2/3}$	8	4	4	1	2
Downs W, 1-0	4	3	0	0	1	1
Bedrosian S,2	$1/3$	1	0	0	1	1

Umpires—Home, Quick; First, Williams; Second, Marsh; Third, Harvey; Left, Froemming; Right, Tata.
T—3:13. A—62,078.

another run in the fourth and Zim brought in Steve Wilson.

We tied the game at four in the fifth. I singled and scored on Mark's triple. Andre followed with a double, scoring Mark, and we were back in it. But that didn't last long. Clark doubled to lead off the Giants' fifth and, after Mitchell flied out, Steve and Matt Williams got locked in a real pitcher-hitter duel. Williams fouled off six pitches with two strikes. Steve was getting his pitches on the corners and Williams managed to keep spoiling them. Then he connected for a two-run homer and the Giants led, 6-4.

Shawon led off the sixth with a bloop hit to right. The next thing we knew, he and Clark were yelling at each other. Both dugouts emptied, but nothing happened. I guess the pitcher, Kelly Downs, was kidding Shawon and asked him if he was going to take a hit like that. Shawon shows his frustration a little more than most and he wasn't in a kidding mood. Later, my infield single got him as far as third, but we couldn't score him.

We had another shot at the Giants in the ninth. With two out, Ryno and Lloyd singled and Mark walked, bringing up Andre. Bedrosian struck him out to end the game.

It was a very tough loss. Again we had chances to win it and didn't deliver. After the game, Zim said that we'd won three in a row before and we honestly thought that, if we could win tomorrow, we'd get them back to Wrigley and beat them in both games there.

October 9

We played hard in Game Five and it didn't happen. But it almost did. Again it was right down to the wire and again we left runners on base ready to score. Again we led early, only to lose late. Going into the bottom of the seventh, we had a 1-0 lead; I scored our run in the third when Ryno doubled me home from second. Mike Bielecki had the Giants shut out on two hits until Clark opened the seventh with a triple and scored on a sacrifice fly by Mitchell to tie the game.

Giants 3, Cubs 2

	ab	r	h	bi		ab	r	h	bi
Butler cf	3	1	0	0	Walton	4	1	2	1
Thompson 2b	3	0	0	0	Sandberg 2b	4	0	1	1
Clark 1b	4	1	3	2	Wynne lf	4	0	1	0
Mitchell lf	2	0	0	1	Grace 1b	3	0	2	0
M. Williams 3b	4	0	1	0	Dawson rf	3	0	0	0
Kennedy c	3	0	0	0	Mi. Williams p	0	0	0	0
Sheridan rf	2	0	0	0	Lancaster p	0	0	0	0
Oberkfell	1	0	0	0	Salazar 3b	4	0	1	0
Bedrosian p	0	0	0	0	Dunston ss	4	0	1	0
Uribe ss	3	0	0	0	Girardi c	3	0	0	0
Reuschel p	2	0	0	0	Wilkerson	1	1	1	0
Maldonado rf	0	1	0	0	Bielecki p	3	0	0	0
					Webster rf	1	0	1	0
Totals	**27**	**3**	**4**	**3**	**Totals**	**34**	**2**	**10**	**2**

```
San Francisco        000  000  12x  —3
CUBS                 001  000  001  —2
```

DP—Giants 2. LOB—CUBS 9, Giants 5. S—Sandberg.
SF—Mitchell. HBP—Dawson by Reuschel. PB—Girardi.

	IP	H	R	ER	BB	SO
Cubs						
Bielecki L, 0-1	$7^{2/3}$	3	3	3	3	8
Mi.Williams	0	1	0	0	0	0
Lancaster	$^{1/3}$	0	0	0	1	0
San Francisco						
Reuschel W, 1-1	8	7	1	0	2	4
Bedrosian S, 3	1	3	1	1	0	0

Umpires—Home, Williams; First, Marsh; Second, Harvey;
Third, Froemming; Left, Tata; Right, Quick.
T—2:47 A—62,084

I was on third with two out in the eighth and they
walked Mark to get to Andre and he grounded back
to the pitcher. In their half of the eighth, with two out,
Mike had control problems and he walked three
straight batters. Zim brought in Mitch to face Clark
with the series on the line. Mitch had him 0-and-2
and then 1-and-2. Then he hit a couple of foul balls.
He hit the next fastball up the middle and two runs
scored, giving the Giants a 3-1 lead. Les came in and
got Matt Williams to end the inning.

The Giants brought in Bedrosian, their closer, in
relief of Reuschel for the top of the ninth. When Luis
and Shawon went out quickly, the fans were on their

feet. Zim had Curtis pinch-hit for Joe Girardi and he singled to left. I thought to myself, "Oh, oh, here we go." Mitch followed with a single to center and I came up figuring I was going to get a hit because I didn't like the alternative. I got one of his fastballs and sent it through the middle, scoring Curtis and putting the tying run at second. Our hopes were kept alive with Ryno at the plate, but he grounded out on the first pitch and it was all over.

A lot of us sat there for a while and watched the Giants celebrate. We knew in our hearts that we had come a lot closer than four games to one indicated. Our team had a .303 team average for the series, but we ran into a few hot bats and we came up a strategic hit or so short in three of our four losses. We knew we had no reason to hang our heads. And I think all of us who watched their victory party knew that it wasn't luck that got us there, that we'd be back and next time everyone else would be watching us do the high-fiving and hugging.

Andre said it for all of us after the game. He said the reason it was his biggest disappointment was because there was no way he believed the Giants were better than the Cubs. The playoffs had to be one of the toughest times in his life. He was in a lot of pain, hurting the whole time. He came over in the outfield and talked to me when we were making pitching changes and told me he was really hurting. I think the pain made it hard for him to concentrate. Andre is a guy who wants to be in there. Everybody, including Andre, felt that he'd come through. He's tough; he wanted to do it. You could tell that it hurt him a lot that he hadn't been able to carry us through a couple of games. Even with bad knees, Andre was a guy who had earned the right to be there and, if we had taken a vote, we would have elected him to the lineup and taken our chances.

After the game, Zim gave us a pep talk and you could tell he really meant it. He told us how proud he was of us and how we had given him the best he had ever had in baseball.

I read later that a couple of writers were blaming Zim for our loss, saying that he forgot the moves that got us there. I don't think he changed his style of managing in the playoff—we just didn't get the hits—or the breaks—when we needed them. If one or two of us had joined Mark and gone on a hot streak the way Clark, Mitchell, and Williams did, we could have won it. And we would have given Oakland more than they could have handled, too.

It was subdued when we boarded the plane for Chicago. While the plane was still on the runway, Mr. Stanton Cook of the Tribune Company came back and talked to us for a few minutes. He told us to hold our heads high; that it had been a great season and, even if we came up a bit short, we could be proud for the rest of our lives of what we had done as a team this year.

I think that helped our mood a lot. After takeoff the guys were going up and down the cabin, congratulating each other on the season and remembering the fun that we had enjoyed together. We swapped phone numbers so that we could stay in touch over the winter. It was the same great closeness that had been there all season. Even though it hurt to lose the playoffs, we were able to seal our good feelings and friendships and get ready for next year. We'd be back...

Epilogue
by Jim Langford

Thinking back on 1984 and other seasons in his life as a player and manager, Jim Frey told Andrew Bagnato of the *Chicago Tribune*, "You get over what happens—you get over the elation of winning or the disappointment of losing in a month. And after a month or so, you look back and say, 'Well, that was a good season.'"

He is right, of course. But Cub fans—and, I suspect, the players as well—will look back on the 1989 season with happy memories that not even a bad ending can diminish.

It was a season that reminded us how important teamwork is, a season of improbable comebacks, hair-raising relief stints, of daring on the basepaths and graceful excellence up the middle. It was a season that displayed a perfect blend of experience and youth and proved again that quiet confidence and positive thinking are the hinges upon which success necessarily relies.

153

Perhaps that was exemplified best as far back as spring training. Dwight Smith was having trouble with his fielding and the flaws were serious enough that he was soon to be assigned to Iowa to work on them. Dwight asked Andre Dawson if he could have one of his gloves. When a player wins a Gold Glove award, he also receives a couple of gloves with a gold label on them. Andre got him one of these special gloves and told him that it had some magic in it. Dwight took some kidding about wearing a gold glove, but Andre's generosity and encouragement, Jimmy Piersall's coaching, and Dwight's hard work produced dramatic improvement in his fielding during the season.

The summer of 1989 supplied illustration for another truth as well—that sometimes apparent adversity can be a friend in disguise. When the entire starting outfield and then the star first baseman and finally the only experienced catcher went down with injuries, the result was not despair or desperation. Instead it presented opportunity to people like Lloyd McClendon, Domingo Ramos, Doug Dascenzo, Joe Girardi, and Rick Wrona, Darrin Jackson, Dwight Smith, and Curtis Wilkerson. And they gave it their best and helped develop the sense that on any given day any one of these guys could come through with the hit or defensive play that would be the margin of victory.

That same adversity brought out the best in Don Zimmer because it made him manage differently than he ever had before. There was no set lineup to pencil in every day as there had been in his heyday with the Red Sox or even on poorer teams where the eight regulars needed to play for there to be any hope of victory. Watching Zimmer this summer gave you the sense that he was working harder than he ever had before and that his more than 40 years in baseball had given him a wealth of experience and honed his instincts to the point where he was exactly the right person to mastermind this team in this campaign. You could see, too, that he was having fun mixing and matching, guessing right on pitchouts, squeezing runs home, manufacturing runs by combining ingredients rather than pleading to his friend and boss Jim Frey for power at all costs. When adversity in the form of injury couldn't fell the Cubs, everybody—the regulars, bench, the manager, and fans—began to realize that we were good, we knew how to play, we could win.

As Jerome Walton comes back to time and again in his account of the season, this team stayed loose by having fun, enjoying themselves, giving and taking the humor that makes even hard work enjoyable.

The playoff loss in 1984 left players and fans with a sense of sadness. It didn't hurt as much this time—maybe because the whole season was so enjoyable not even that ending could spoil it—maybe because we are so used to this team coming back from a poor series to go on a winning streak that we know it will come even if we have to wait until April.

It is fun to see the difference a year makes in how the press views the Cubs. Don Zimmer received 23 of 24 first-place votes in being name National League Manager of the Year by the Baseball Writers Association of America. A headline in *USA Today* announces, "CUBS COULD BE EVEN STRONGER NEXT SEASON." Another, in the *Chicago Tribune,* says simply, "CUBS OUT TO FILL A FEW HOLES." The youth that a year ago was rated as a Cub weakness now suddenly is a strength. The general manager, targeted for criticism last December and again prior to the stretch drive, now is portrayed as bold and wise. And Jerome Walton, the question mark from Double-A Pittsfield, is now acknowledged, as Jimmy

Piersall predicted he would be, as one of the best centerfielders in the league. A poll of players conducted by *USA Today* had him second only to Eric Davis as the best centerfielder in the National League. He is also one of the best leadoff hitters in the league. In the 113 games he started, he led off by reaching base 40 times and scored 21 runs in the first inning. The Cubs won 16 of the 21 times he did so. He had 18 bunt hits this year and four of them came on two-strike counts. Only once did he bunt foul for a third strike.

As I came to know Jerome Walton in the course of working on this book with him, the thing that impressed me most about him is his inner strength. He is physically very talented—blessed with great speed, balance, reactions, and instinct. But it is what he has done with those talents that sets him apart. He plays fluidly but under control; if he makes a mistake he learns from it; he doesn't put pressure on himself; he is quiet but friendly; he loves humor and wit. His work ethic and determination promise success at whatever he does. Although he grew up without a father, he has been blessed with a mother, grandmother, and grandfather who shared their values and love with him in a way that guided him but also allowed him the freedom to grow by his own choices. He is religious in a deep and personal way.

Jerome's ambition is to play in the major leagues for another 15 years, most of them with the Cubs and maybe the last two closer to home with the Braves, the team he followed while growing up. When his playing days are over, he wants to coach—in high school or college—and clearly that is to give to someone else the instruction and encouragement that his coaches gave him.

In late October, Jerome came to South Bend for a couple of days to finish our collaboration on this book. Knowing Juice had played football in high school, we thought he'd enjoy watching the Notre Dame football team as they prepared for an upcoming game with Pittsburgh. We asked Notre Dame coach Lou Holtz if we could come out to watch a late afternoon practice. It was a wonderful experience. Coach Holtz personally welcomed Jerome and congratulated him on his outstanding season and the players were yelling over greetings and waving to him. Coach asked him to stay until the end of practice and to say a few words to the team. When the time came, the players gathered, Coach introduced Jerome, and he gave a very short but moving few sentences: "Be grateful to the Lord for your talent. Work hard. Believe in yourself. Have fun and be together." Holtz concluded he couldn't have said it better himself. Then everyone joined hands, knelt down, and said a silent prayer. That brief speech really summed up Jerome Walton.

On November 8, the vote of the Baseball Writers Association of America was announced and Jerome Walton was named National League Rookie of the Year by a large margin over teammate and best friend Dwight Smith. Even though the announcement came on Dwight's birthday, Jerome cracked, "I'm glad he is runner-up." It was the first time a Cub had won the honor since Ken Hubbs did it in 1962 and only once before in the National League have teammates finished 1-2 in the voting. That was in 1957 when Jack Sanford and Ed Bouchee did it with the Phillies.

Jerome was glad to win the award. He doesn't expect a sophomore jinx. Instead he has his goals already set: a .300 batting average, more stolen bases, and a World Championship for the Cubs. Don't bet against it!

CUBS BATTING STATISTICS*

PLAYER	AVG.	G	AB	R	H	TB	2B	3B	HR	RBI	HP	BB	SO	SB	CS	E	SLG	OBP
Berryhill, D	.257	91	334	37	86	114	13	0	5	41	2	16	54	1	0	4	.341	.291
RIGHT	.340		97		33	47	5	0	3	13	0	4	8				.485	.359
LEFT	.224		237		53	67	8	0	2	28	2	12	46				.283	.264
+Dascenzo, D	.165	47	139	20	23	27	1	0	1	12	0	13	13	6	3	0	.194	.234
RIGHT	.197		61		12	12	0	0	0	5	0	4	4				.197	.242
LEFT	.141		78		11	15	1	0	1	7	0	9	9				.192	.227
Dawson, A	.252	118	416	62	105	198	18	6	21	77	1	35	62	8	5	3	.476	.307
Dunston, S	.278	138	471	52	131	190	20	6	9	60	1	30	86	19	11	17	.403	.320
+Girardi, J	.248	59	157	15	39	52	10	0	1	14	2	11	26	2	1	7	.331	.304
Grace, M	.314	142	510	74	160	233	28	3	13	79	0	80	42	14	7	6	.457	.405
Law, V	.235	130	408	38	96	145	22	3	7	42	0	38	73	2	2	13	.355	.296
McClendon, L	.286	92	259	47	74	124	12	1	12	40	1	37	31	6	4	6	.479	.368
Ramos, D	.263	85	179	18	47	60	6	2	1	19	2	17	23	1	1	11	.335	.333
Salazar, L	.282	121	326	34	92	135	12	2	9	34	1	15	57	1	4	10	.414	.316
CHI	.325	26	80	7	26	34	5	0	1	12	0	4	13	0	1	3	.425	.357
Sandberg, R	.290	157	606	104	176	301	25	5	30	76	4	59	85	15	5	6	.497	.356
+Smith, D	.324	109	343	52	111	169	19	6	9	52	2	31	51	9	4	5	.493	.382
+Smith, G	.400	4	5	1	2	2	0	0	0	2	1	0	0	0	0	2	.400	.500
RIGHT	.000		1		0	0	0	0	0	0	0	0	0				.000	.000
LEFT	.500		4		2	2	0	0	0	2	1	0	0				.500	.600

CUBS BATTING STATISTICS Cont.*

PLAYER	AVG.	G	AB	R	H	TB	2B	3B	HR	RBI	HP	BB	SO	SB	CS	E	SLG	OBP
Varsho, G	.184	61	87	10	16	24	4	2	0	6	0	4	13	3	0	2	.276	.220
+Walton, J	.293	116	475	64	139	183	23	3	5	46	6	27	77	24	7	3	.385	.335
Webster, M	.257	98	272	40	70	99	12	4	3	19	1	30	55	14	2	6	.364	.331
RIGHT	.311		61		19	27	3	1	1	2	0	5	9				.443	.364
LEFT	.242		211		51	72	9	3	2	17	1	25	46				.341	.322
Wilkerson, C	.244	77	160	18	39	50	4	2	1	10	0	8	33	4	2	8	.313	.278
RIGHT	.171		41		7	11	1	0	1	3	0	2	7				.268	.209
LEFT	.269		119		32	39	3	2	0	7	0	6	26				.328	.302
+Wrona, R	.283	38	92	11	26	36	2	1	2	14	1	2	21	0	0	3	.391	.299
Wynne, M	.243	125	342	27	83	121	13	2	7	39	2	13	48	6	1	6	.354	.274
CHI	.188	20	48	8	9	16	2	1	1	4	1	1	7	2	0	1	.333	.220
CHICAGO	.261	162	5513	702	1438	2135	235	45	124	653	26	472	921	136	57	122	.387	.319
OPPONENTS	.250	162	5483	623	1369	1997	244	33	106	577	25	532	918	86	56	155	.364	.317

+ Denotes Rookies

* Compiled by the MLB-IBM BASEBALL INFORMATION SYSTEM

CUBS PITCHING STATISTICS*

PLAYER	R/L	W	L	ERA	G	GS	CG	GF	SHO	SV	IP	H	R	ER	HR	HB	BB	IBB	SO	WP	BK	OPP AVG
Assenmacher, P	L	3	4	3.99	63	0	0	17	0	0	76.2	74	37	34	3	1	28	8	79	3	1	.255
CHI	L	2	1	5.21	14	0	0	3	0	0	19.0	19	11	11	1	0	12	1	15	0	0	.275
Bielecki, M	R	18	7	3.14	33	33	4	0	3	0	212.1	187	82	74	16	0	81	8	147	9	4	.237
+Blankenship, K	R	0	0	1.69	2	0	0	1	0	0	5.1	4	1	1	0	0	2	0	2	0	0	.200
Kilgus, P	L	6	10	4.39	35	23	0	5	0	2	145.2	164	90	71	9	5	49	6	61	3	2	.283
Lancaster, L	R	4	2	1.36	42	0	0	15	0	8	72.2	60	12	11	2	0	15	1	56	2	1	.226
Maddux, G	R	19	12	2.95	35	35	7	0	1	0	238.1	222	90	78	13	6	82	13	135	5	3	.249
Perry, P	L	0	1	1.77	19	0	0	6	0	1	35.2	23	8	7	2	0	16	3	20	1	0	.187
Pico, J	R	3	1	3.77	53	5	0	17	0	2	90.2	99	43	38	8	0	31	10	38	2	0	.278
Sanderson, S	R	11	9	3.94	37	23	2	2	0	0	146.1	155	69	64	16	2	31	6	86	1	3	.274
Sutcliffe, R	R	16	11	3.66	35	34	5	0	1	0	229.0	202	98	93	18	2	69	8	153	12	6	.240
+Wilkins, D	R	1	0	4.60	11	0	0	1	0	0	15.2	13	9	8	2	0	9	2	14	0	0	.228
Williams, M	L	4	4	2.76	76	0	0	61	0	36	81.2	71	27	25	6	8	52	4	67	6	4	.238
+Wilson, S	L	6	4	4.20	53	8	0	9	0	2	85.2	83	43	40	6	1	31	5	65	0	1	.257
CHICAGO		93	69	3.43	162	162	18	144	10	55	1460.1	1369	623	556	106	25	532	70	918	44	24	.250
OPPONENTS		69	93	3.84	162	162	17	145	12	35	1448.2	1438	702	618	124	26	472	75	921	58	18	.261

+ Denotes Rookies
* Compiled by the MLB-IBM BASEBALL INFORMATION SYSTEM

CUBS PLAYOFF STATISTICS

BATTING

CUBS	AB	R	H	2B	3B	HR	RBI	AVG.
McCldn lf-c	3	0	2	0	0	0	0	.667
Grace 1b	17	3	11	3	1	1	8	.647
Wilkersn 3b	2	1	1	0	0	0	0	.500
Sutcliffe p	2	0	1	1	0	0	0	.500
Sandberg 2b	20	6	8	3	1	1	4	.400
Salazar 3b	19	2	7	0	1	1	2	.368
Walton cf	22	4	8	0	0	0	2	.364
Webster lf-rf	3	0	1	0	0	0	0	.333
Dunston ss	19	2	6	0	0	0	0	.316
Smith lf	15	2	3	1	0	0	0	.200
Bielecki p	5	0	1	0	0	0	2	.200
Wynne cf-lf	6	0	1	0	0	0	0	.167
Dawson rf	19	0	2	1	0	0	3	.105
Girardi c	10	1	1	0	0	0	0	.100
Wrona c	5	0	0	0	0	0	0	.000
Maddux p	3	1	0	0	0	0	0	.000
Law 3b	3	0	0	0	0	0	0	.000
Lancaster p	1	0	0	0	0	0	0	.000
Wilson p	0	0	0	0	0	0	0	.000
Assnmchr p	0	0	0	0	0	0	0	.000
Kilgus p	0	0	0	0	0	0	0	.000
Ramos ph	1	0	0	0	0	0	0	.000
Sanderson p	0	0	0	0	0	0	0	.000
M.Willms p	0	0	0	0	0	0	0	.000
Totals	**175**	**22**	**53**	**9**	**3**	**3**	**21**	**.303**

PITCHING

CUBS	G	IP	H	R	ER	BB	SO	ERA
Kilgus	1	3	4	0	0	1	1	0.00
Sanderson	1	2	2	0	0	0	1	0.00
M.Willms	2	1	1	0	0	0	2	0.00
Bielecki 0-1	2	12.1	7	5	5	6	11	3.65
Sutcliffe	1	6	5	3	3	4	2	4.50
Wilson 0-1	2	3.2	3	5	2	1	4	4.91
Lncstr 1-1	3	6	6	4	4	1	3	6.35
Maddux 0-1	2	7.1	13	12	11	4	5	13.50
Assnmchr	2	.2	3	1	1	0	0	13.50
Totals	**5**	**42**	**44**	**30**	**26**	**17**	**29**	**5.57**

Score by Innings

San Francisco		703 720 371—30
Cubs		(11)12 123 101—22

NL ROOKIE OF THE YEAR VOTING

PLAYER	1st	2nd	3rd	Total
Jerome Walton, CUBS — — — — —	22	2	—	116
Dwight Smith, CUBS — — — — — —	2	19	1	68
Gregg Jefferies, N.Y. — — — — — — —	—	1	15	18
Derek Lilliquist, Atlanta — — — — —	—	1	3	6
Andy Benes, San Diego — — — — — —	—	—	3	3
Charlie Hayes, Philadelphia — — —	—	1	—	3
Greg Harris, San Diego — — — — —	—	—	2	2